D0734532

THE MINISTER
AS CRISIS COUNSELOR

THE MINISTER
AS CRISIS COUNSELOR

David K. Switzer

Nashville · ABINGDON PRESS · New York

THE MINISTER AS CRISIS COUNSELOR

Copyright © 1974 by Abingdon Press

Library of Congress Cataloging in Publication Data

SWITZER, DAVID K. 1925-
   The minister as crisis counselor. 1. Pastoral
counseling. I. Title.
BV4012.2.S9   253.5   73-13722

ISBN 0-687-26953-9

Scripture quotations unless otherwise noted are from the Revised
Standard Version of the Bible, copyrighted 1946, 1952, and 1971
by the Division of Christian Education, National Council of Churches,
and are used by permission.

MANUFACTURED BY THE PARTHENON PRESS AT
NASHVILLE, TENNESSEE, UNITED STATES OF AMERICA

TO
Shirley
Rebecca
Eric

PREFACE

Some books are deliberately planned by the authors. Others seem merely to accumulate. This book falls into the latter category. After my first introduction to crisis theory and methods of intervention some eight years ago, I kept waiting for someone to write a book on this subject specifically directed toward the clergyman, so much of whose work is with persons and families in crisis. In the meantime, my own file began to grow as I put together articles, lectures, workshop notes, until finally there was a stack of material that seemed to say, in the absence of the book by someone else—"Put me together."

Over these several years there has been an increasing literature dealing with crisis. For the most part, however, the references have been short articles in many different professional journals and parts of books, most of which have been quite unknown and inaccessible to the minister. Very few of these have sought to pull together in any comprehensive manner the relevant data for understanding both the theory and the functioning throughout the helping process. In addition, except for a single issue of *Pastoral Psychology*, they have not been directed toward the minister.

There was almost a total lack of published resources in the area of crisis for the practicing clergyman. Therefore, in spite of the agonies of writing and the fact that

I did not have any time off from my regular responsibilities at Perkins School of Theology, I added to my already available material the selected results of a rather thorough research of the professional journals from the time articles on crisis began to be published. A few books were examined and the process of putting it all together began. Here it is. Other books are bound to follow, and I welcome them. In fact, I would have welcomed them much earlier. But we ministers clearly need to develop our own insights and styles of functioning in crisis and share these with one another. As we do so we may discover that we have something to offer to other professionals who also operate in the alleviation of crisis, just as they have contributed and are contributing to us. In fact, I would suppose that several of the chapters of this book would be quite applicable to any mental health professional or even any lay person who is in a setting where he is called upon to be a crisis counselor.

My total thank-you list is too long to be published. I shall try, though, to point out major areas of indebtedness. My own specific introduction to crisis theory and intervention came in a course offered to clergymen by the Los Angeles County Department of Mental Health and the Mental Health and Clergy Committee of Los Angeles. Many of these leaders' names are found in the footnotes. My fear is that some of their material, which got into my head from their lectures and our discussions, might have found its way into the text of two of my chapters without appropriate reference as I assimilated in my own practice and thinking what they were teaching me. Let this then be the reference as well as my expression of appreciation.

Some of this book already has a public history. Parts

of chapters 2 and 3 were first a very brief article in the *Christian Advocate* and later a longer article in *Pastoral Psychology*. Chapter 6 was published with only slight variations in *Omega*: An International Journal for the Psychological Study of Dying, Death, Bereavement, Suicide, and Other Lethal Behaviors. The editors of these journals have given permission for the publication of the articles in revised form here.

Several years spent training lay persons to do telephone crisis intervention at Contact and Suicide Prevention Center, both twenty-four-hour telephone counseling services in Dallas, gave feedback on the practical usefulness of the approach utilized here; and an invitation to give two presentations on crisis theory and therapy as a part of the Timberlawn Psychiatric Residency Program Guest Lecture Series provided the opportunity to test the ideas and organization of chapters 2 and 3 with a sophisticated audience and contributed to their final shape. Chapter 5 was developed originally as a lecture to the Southwest Regional Interseminary Movement Conference in 1972, with additional research adding to its form in this book.

I thought it to be of crucial importance to include an emphasis on the family as the context of most crises, and especially on divorce. Because of my own lack of research in this area, and feeling some sense of urgency in getting the book to press, I felt fortunate to have as close personal friends and colleagues two highly competent professionals, Dr. W. Robert Beavers, a psychiatrist, and Dr. Richard Hunt, a minister and psychologist, who were quite capable of immediately developing the two chapters on these topics.

Frequent reference is made throughout the book to the therapeutic strategy of gathering the family together:

the frequent need of doing so in order to avoid some of the potentially destructive effects of an inadequately resolved crisis (such as grief) on the whole family, or certain individuals in the family, and the potency of drawing upon the resources of the family unit with a view to strengthening a single member in crisis.

If the minister is not aware of the fact that the family is a complex system which has developed its own patterns of maintaining itself, that these systems differ radically, and that whole family units do not respond in identical ways to his interventions, then he is less likely to experience consistent success as a crisis counselor. He must be able to identify the differing systems and allow his understanding of their degrees of openness, forms of communication, and mechanisms of defense and self-maintenance to guide his own flexible functioning as a therapeutic agent in their family crisis.

It is for this reason that Dr. Beavers has written about systems theory and its application to three major categories of family functioning, recognizing that it is within these families that persons are created, that it is usually within the context of some type of family organization that individuals experience crises, and that whole families can be in crisis.

Because of the particular balance of a family system and the type of interactions and identifications that are involved in maintaining the persons within it, it seems rather obvious that any major disruption or breakup of the family will ordinarily produce a sense of threat to the individuals involved.

In addition, we should not overlook the prevalence of divorce as a common form of family breakup and the fact that the minister is frequently involved with the pre- and postdivorce crises of persons. The chapter by

Dr. Hunt speaks directly to the issue of the total marriage disintegration process, beginning in the midst of the marriage itself, moving to the point of decision to divorce, the time of the actual separation, and the interim following. Specific guidelines for the minister's functioning are detailed in relation to each of these periods.

In addition to the assistance from professional colleagues, I must also acknowledge that of my wife, Shirley—herself a skilled crisis counselor, first as a volunteer in California and Texas, and now also a professional—who, through the recounting of her experiences and insights, has continued to stimulate my own thinking and practice.

I am particularly blessed in having had a competent and good-spirited secretary, Mrs. Gladys Mollet, who has not only typed (and retyped) the manuscript, but has proofread the copy and developed the Index of Names. There must be a special place in heaven for such people.

Finally, I continue to remember with affection the staff and congregation of the First United Methodist Church of Pasadena, California, who provided the context in which my new learning and skills in crisis intervention first began to be applied. Especially am I grateful to those persons who allowed me to participate with them in their struggles in times of stress, anxiety, and pain. I also want to express the same to those students of Perkins School of Theology and members of their families who have either sought me out or responded to my initiative with openness, sharing intimate details of their own feelings of distress and trouble in such a way that their crises have been resolved, and have contributed at the same time to my own growth as a human being and a professional. These relationships have developed into continuing friendships of great meaning.

David K. Switzer

CONTENTS

Chapter I

THE MINISTER
AS CRISIS COUNSELOR

In one way or another, the Christian pastor throughout the centuries has been involved with persons in time of crisis and distress. He has always in this sense been a counselor. This is hardly news to anyone who might be reading this book. Nor is there in these days a setting in which an ordained minister may work where he is not called upon, at least occasionally, to engage himself with someone who is hurting in some way. Certainly in the local pastorate and in many specialized ministries the demand is constant. He may seek this form of pastoral work or attempt to avoid it; he may be well or poorly trained for it; he may do it effectively or rather badly. But there is no escape from the counseling responsibility short of escape from the ministry itself. Actually, most ministers place a high value on the importance of their role as pastors and the helping relationship with persons and feel that this is one of the most satisfying activities in which they participate.[1]

[1] Samuel Blizzard, "The Minister's Dilemma," *The Christian Century*, April 25, 1956. Although this is now an old study, and new items would need to be added to the list of ministers' functions, there is no reason to believe that the emphasis on pastoral work (with counseling perhaps now being specified as one aspect of this) would be reduced. If anything, I would expect an increased value to be placed on it.

WHAT IS PASTORAL COUNSELING?

If we take the professional psychotherapist as a model for comparison, the minister is a strange kind of counselor indeed, and he comes to this function by a professionally circuitous route. In order to get to the point of understanding the minister as crisis counselor, it may be enlightening to look first at the unique meaning of the term "pastoral counselor." Perhaps a diagram will be helpful.

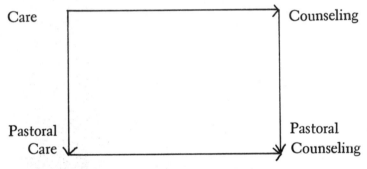

Care   Counseling

Pastoral   Pastoral
Care   Counseling

Tillich has properly pointed out the nature of caring as a general and universal human characteristic. As he puts it, caring "is going on always in every moment of human existence." [2] Caring is transformed into pastoral care by reference both to motivation and context. It is the conscious acting out toward one another of the love that God has shown to us in Jesus Christ, and it is done within and also as a representative of the community of faith. This moves us in one direction beyond the general human characteristic of care as another dimension is added to it.

[2] Paul Tillich, "The Spiritual and Theological Foundations of Pastoral Care," in *Clinical Education for the Pastoral Ministry*, E. E. Bruder and M. L. Barb, eds. (Advisory Commmittee on Clinical Pastoral Education, 1958), p. 1.

But there are certain types of situations of human distress for which the general human quality of caring, or even pastoral caring, is not sufficient to produce healing. Therefore, specialized techniques of caring have been developed which have the potential to produce change in human life even when there are deep and persistent problems. This kind of caring is called counseling or psychotherapy. Thus, another dimension is added in another direction to the everyday mutual caring of persons for one another.

Now, moving from the position of counseling in the direction of the pastoral motivation and context, and from the position of pastoral care in the direction of the function of specialized counseling, we find that the intersection of the lines indicates what the minister is doing when he engages in pastoral counseling.

Counseling "in General"

Even though in many ways the pastoral counselor may be distinguished from the situation and functioning of the professional psychotherapist, there are certain aspects of the counseling process and relationship that are identical, no matter who the counselor might be, if effective counseling is taking place. At the risk of being trite, perhaps the word counseling itself should be further clarified. Let it be understood from the very beginning that no one particular methodology is intended. Although there are methods and techniques, there is no single way to counsel. Counseling is a relational process. It is being a person to and for another person. It is providing a model of personhood in contrast to an emphasis on techniques. Even Karl Menninger as a psychoanalyst writes, "In my opinion the most

17

important thing in the acquisition of psychoanalytic technique is the development of a certain attitude or frame of mind." [3] And Theodore Reik, another psychoanalyst, emphasizes the point in what really must be something of an overstatement that there are no techniques, only persons. I say overstatement because, certainly within the ministry, which may occasionally be inclined toward the error of overemphasizing this particular aspect of truth to the exclusion of the counterbalances necessary for it to *be* the truth, it is important to avoid the overly simplistic, erroneous, and potentially harmful conclusion that "because I'm such a great guy whom everyone automatically loves, I am a highly competent counselor." This is, of course, not necessarily so. Still, with this corrective statement, the *human* element is at the center of the counseling process.

Robert Carkhuff, building upon the work of Carl Rogers and carrying it farther, states as a result of extensive research with clients that there are several essential ingredients of effective psychotherapy. One of these is genuineness. [4] He is referring to the counselor's own genuineness as a person, his capacity to be in touch with himself, aware of what is going on in himself at any given moment, and his ability to communicate himself, not merely his ideas, clearly and appropriately to others. Jourard is traveling the same route when he speaks of "real-self interpersonal behavior" and *"being in the presence of another."* [5] This implies patterns of behavior with others in which one person relates with-

[3] Karl Menninger, *Theory of Psychoanalytic Technique* (New York: Basic Books, 1958), p. 10.
[4] Robert Carkhuff, *Helping and Human Relations*, 2 vols. (New York: Holt, Rinehart and Winston, 1969), Vol. I, pp. 184-87.
[5] Sidney Jourard, *The Transparent Self* (Princeton, N.J.: Van Nostrand, 1964), pp. 59-65.

out anxiety or defensiveness so that the anxiety of the other is reduced, barriers to self-disclosure are removed, and self-disclosure itself is facilitated. Such a form of relating is what provides the atmosphere for change, because the process of self-revealing is that which is inherently healing in the person. Jourard's point is that a person is healthy to the degree that he is open, to the degree that he allows himself to be transparent to others. The masked, the self-enclosed counselor (or for that matter, preacher) is a contradiction in terms.

Counseling is acceptance and love of another. It is the facilitation of communication—communication being not just the use of words, even intellectually precise ones—but the art of understanding and being understood. This includes emotional meanings as well as intellectual ones. It is quite clear from this that the counselor is not merely a detached observer of a process but rather a related participant, albeit more objective than the other person, though not totally objective, since there is no such thing. Sullivan uses the term "participant-observer" to describe the therapist's role.[6] Counseling is entering into a dynamic process. It is giving one's time, therefore sharing a part of one's life with another, reliving part of his life along with him, entering into new life with him. A counselor certainly should avoid getting caught in the same emotional trap in which the counselee finds himself, but he does enter into the other person's emotional world with him. The counselor is a mirror for the other. But he is more than that. He not only reflects feelings, he feels. He not only reflects meaning, he participates in the creation of

[6] Harry Stack Sullivan, *The Psychiatric Interview* (New York: W. W. Norton & Co., 1954), pp. 19-25.

meaning. He is not the aggressive molder of another individual into a preconceived pattern, but he is not neutral about the outcome of the process either. He is committed to the person with whom he is involved. Yet his own selfhood must never be threatened by the failure of the other to respond as the counselor feels he should.

All this is to say that counseling is a dynamic personal relationship in which both persons participate and both persons change. Even in what we might judge failure, the counselee is not unaffected, nor is the counselor ever left unchanged. He gains insights, recognizes his own responses, learns from the other, and is himself confronted by the other.

The Uniqueness of the Minister as Counselor

In talking about counseling in these terms, however, there is nothing at all unique about the minister. Nevertheless, there are a number of ways in which the clergyman *is* quite distinct from other psychotherapists. Actually, it is not at all clear that the professional psychotherapist should be our primary model any more than the premodern minister should be. In fact, there are already in process of development new models that are something of a fusion of the two, and one of these is precisely what this whole book seeks to elaborate. This new model is one that is in keeping with the pastor's traditional role throughout the centuries and very much related to the rather extensive involvement with persons given to him by his role as a minister of a local congregation. At the same time, it also includes a technical knowledge of personality dynamics, psychopathology, and contemporary counseling approaches.

Because of the minister's role, he comes much closer to total involvement therapeutically with larger numbers of persons with a greater variety of problems than any psychologist or psychiatrist. As contrasted with these professionals, the minister either knows to some degree a relatively high percentage of people with whom he engages in counseling, or he will have some form of continuing extraoffice relationship with them, a point that will be referred to later. Most psychiatrists and psychologists are rarely involved directly in a helping way with grief situations, premarital counseling, supportive counseling of the physically ill and the dying, the most frequent problems of aging, or even with suicide and alcoholism in ways of functioning that are open to a clergyman. Yet the minister is, or should be, almost always significantly related to persons in these situations. In addition, there are other ways in which the clergyman is quite distinct from other psychotherapists, and these particularly contribute to his potential effectiveness in situations of crisis: his symbol power, what might be called pastoral initiative, his prior personal relationship with many of the persons into whose lives he enters now in this unique relationship, the availability and value of the community of faith. There are also such aids as the growing practice and acceptance of the role of the laity in pastoral care with the minister as teacher-supervisor, and the increase in telephone counseling that are peculiarly available to the clergyman. These will be discussed in later chapters.

The symbol power of the minister. The first and, in my thinking, primary uniqueness of the minister, and one that is a source of peculiar strength in his relationships apart from the power of personal presence, is

21

his power as a symbol. [7] The fact that the counselor is a *minister* is a datum that usually has some impact upon a person. Every professional with clients (or in this instance parishioners) is not only who he is but who the other person feels him to be, not only at a level of conscious awareness but also of unconscious process. He is not only a person but a symbol.

Tillich lists a number of characteristics of symbols in the context of his declaration that "man's ultimate concern must be expressed symbolically, because symbol alone is able to express the ultimate." [8] The first characteristic is the most obvious one, that a symbol points beyond itself to something else. Second, however, unlike a simple sign, a symbol participates in that to which it points. There is somehow a direct, inseparable relationship between the two. The third characteristic of symbol is that it opens up levels of reality that otherwise are closed for us. And fourth, it also unlocks dimensions and elements of our inner being that correspond to the dimensions and elements of reality. What Tillich seems to be expressing here, without using this sort of language, is that, as a result of the symbol's participation in the reality to which it points, it also has the power to communicate something of that reality to the person for whom the symbol is meaningful. [9]

The ordained clergyman must be aware that he himself is a symbol of the reality that underlies the meaningfulness of Christian faith. In other words, quite apart from his own being as a person, the clergyman is per-

---

[7] For another discussion of the minister as a symbol, see Wayne Oates, *The Christian Pastor* (Philadelphia: Westminster Press, 1964), pp. 43-71.

[8] Paul Tillich, *Dynamics of Faith* (New York: Harper & Bros., 1957) p. 41.

[9] *Ibid.*, pp. 41-43.

ceived by others as being the physical representation to the community of faith and, at least to some extent, to the larger community of the reality of God. His very physical presence has the power to stimulate those internal images which, through early learning in a highly emotionally charged relationship of dependence, have become a part of an individual's intrapersonal dynamics. These primitive images are a part of that individual's internal resources and are strong unconscious forces affecting every aspect of his life.[10] Now to be sure, it must be recognized that in the development of quite a number of people these images have negative forces attached to them, but even in many of these people, as well as in a large number of others who have been related to a religious community, they are positive. The clergyman is a physical representation of the whole community of faith, of the tradition, of a way of viewing the meaning of life, of the dynamic power of faith, and of God himself. This is a significant factor not to be overlooked when the minister engages in counseling or intervenes in crises. Because of this symbol power, there may be unconscious negative forces to be dealt with, worked through, and overcome, as well as unconscious positive forces that actually become available to many persons in a strengthening and healing way during their time of distress. While other mental health professionals are also symbols, because of the long-term history of religious communities, the relationship between religion and culture, and the total expo-

---

[10] This understanding of the power of certain symbols as conveying unusual impact upon human life when they have been learned early in life and in relationship with one's parents is based upon the concepts of "good" and "bad" objects, proposed by Melanie Klein, "Mourning and Its Relation to Manic-Depressive States," *International Journal of Psychoanalysis*, XXI (1940), 127-28.

sure of many persons when they are children to the religious community, its collection of symbols, its ritual, and its ministry, and the way in which all of this exposure is integrally tied into the nuclear family itself, the symbol of the pastor seems to be of a different order in terms of its strength.

Pastoral initiative. Another aspect of the uniqueness of the clergyman as a counselor may be termed pastoral initiative, both as it relates to the establishment of pre-counseling relationships and to active crisis intervention. This is an aspect of the minister's functioning that too many all too often take for granted, although all clergymen utilize it more or less consciously in a variety of ways. A minister is rare among professionals in that he is expected to go where people are, and at least usually he will have some entrée. Our social forms have provided this type of expectation, and it is a significant one when utilized sensitively and responsibly in the establishment of precounseling relationships, in active intervention in crisis, and in the follow-up which plays such an important role in crisis counseling. It also allows the freedom to schedule more or less formal counseling appointments in the home of the persons involved rather than in the office, something which a few marriage and family therapists are beginning to do with considerable success and satisfaction. Home, hospital, and job visitation can give a minister a breadth and depth of relationships, an opportunity to know people and be known by them that no psychiatrist or psychologist can match. These visits in themselves occasionally turn rather quickly into brief or even longer counseling sessions. Certainly they provide an excellent basis for a person's calling later on the minister for help, or for the minister's later returning on his own initiative when he feels that his presence can be helpful or supportive. With his entrée to the homes of his people, he is able to discover through sensitive questioning and responsive listening a number of problems that are in their early stages of development. In this way, he may be useful to persons in preventing the development of more serious problems. It is interesting that after all these centuries of this tradition in the ministry, there are a few places where psychiatric emergency teams are beginning to call in people's homes and where teams are being sent to the families of persons who have committed or attempted suicide.

It is also interesting to note the way in which the minister is expected to intervene in certain crisis situations by his own initiative and without specific invitation. He certainly is expected to do so in the matter of physical illness and the situation of grief. People may tend to be somewhat more surprised if he also turns up when someone has gotten drunk or there is a family fight going on. There is an obvious danger in using initiative in these unexpected ways. He may on some occasions be resented and resisted and even rejected. He may in fact fail, and no one likes to fail. But there are also tremendous possibilities for service. Many times in the midst of great stress there is a sense of relief upon the appearance of the minister. Perhaps an individual or family had not even thought of calling him, but his presence is genuinely welcomed. On other occasions, even where there is initial resistance to intrusion, barriers can sometimes be broken down, relationship established or reestablished, and constructive interaction take place. Certainly at times like this the depth and quality of a prior relationship is of major significance. The degree of trust, confidence, sincerity, genuine helpfulness, real friendship make it possible for the pastor's intervention by his own initiative into the crisis to be of a constructive nature. Even where there may be resistance and rejection, it should not be assumed that the intervention is without its unseen positive effects.

Relationships with persons. A third way in which a clergyman is different from professional psychotherapists is that in many of the settings where he functions, he frequently has a prior relationship with a person, an ongoing, out-of-therapy relationship during the span of the counseling, as well as a continuing relationship when the counseling itself is concluded. There are, of course, some exceptions, but it is often the case that the person or persons in need of help are parishioners, fellow workers, friends, neighbors. Some of the implications of this have already been referred to in terms of the possibilities for preventing the growth of more serious problems and the quality of uninvited intervention. In addition, the prior and continuing relationship has implications both for the development of transference and for the usual ways of working through separation at the conclusion of counseling.

Transference, in its simplest terms, refers to the situation in which a person in therapy, without being aware of it, "transfers" onto the therapist feelings originally directed toward the parents and now repressed. These may be hostility, love (including sexual feelings), and dependence, often with the expectation of magical omnipotence. In traditional psychoanalysis, where the analyst is theoretically a neutral figure—not known as a person before, during, or after the therapy—such

26

transference of repressed feeling is invited. Where there has been a prior relationship, as in the case of parishioner and minister, although there may already be some elements of transference growing out of the minister's position and how the parishioner unconsciously views this, the minister is also known as a person, and he continues to be known as a person in contacts outside of the counseling sessions. Under these circumstances, the depth and strength of transference may be reduced.

In addition, the fact that there will be a continuing relationship after the counseling is completed means that termination of counseling does not produce the sharp and absolute loss of relationship, but rather a transformation from one form to another. Recognizing that a parishioner in such an intimate relationship may in fact view it as a loss, still when this perception and the feelings attached to it are verbalized, there are important and potentially quite positive and meaningful carry-over values into the relationship that continues to exist.

The community of faith. An obviously unique resource which the minister has as crisis counselor is the availability and value of the community of faith. In the first place, there are the precounseling advantages. In the education program, in preaching, and in the quality and forms of relating to persons in business meetings and the variety of other small groups, the minister has the opportunity to invite people in indirect ways to come to him for counseling. He also has the opportunity to train people in the art of the anticipation and identification of problems in their early stages and how to deal with them when they arise. No other professional person regularly has this sort of platform

or organizational context in which to do sound education for mental health and problem-solving or to open
doors for people to see him. Beyond this, there is the
supportive community which forms a strengthening
context for many people who are in individual or marriage or family counseling with the minister as they
continue to participate in the life of the community of
which they are already a part. When crises arise, they
are already actually in the midst of many of the resources they will need. For those who come to the
minister from outside the church, there is the community into which at least some of them may be effectively integrated as an additional resource for
strength. Especially are the small group structures helpful at this point, and the value of those that are oriented
for content and fellowship and spiritual life ought not
to be overlooked. There is also the possibility of developing, as many churches have already done, the unstructured small groups of a semitherapeutic or therapeutic
nature which form the social context for a person's testing of his insights and new forms of relating as they
arise during individual counseling.[11]

PASTORAL COUNSELING
AND SECULAR PSYCHOTHERAPY

Many of the first generation leaders of the modern
pastoral care movement, those who sought to bring to
the unique role of the minister the insights and
methodology of certain forms of contemporary psycho-

[11] Howard Clinebell, *The People Dynamic: Changing Self and
Society Through Growth Groups* (New York: Harper & Row, 1972);
Joe Knowles, *Group Counseling* (Englewood Cliffs, N.J.: Prentice-
Hall, 1964); Robert Leslie, *Sharing Groups in the Church* (Nashville:
Abingdon Press, 1971).

therapy, are still with us. It was only shortly before World War II that the work of a number of persons in this new field began to be represented in the curricula of several theological seminaries, and only after the war did the demand for and the availability of competent teachers begin to come together in such a way that pastoral counseling began to move in the direction of becoming the expected and accepted part of seminary education that it is today.

The undergirding theoretical-practical approach, already in the process of being developed by Dicks, Cabot, Hiltner, and others, was supported and stimulated by secular counseling in the work of Carl Rogers.[12] While modern methods of pastoral counseling were not directly derived from Rogers initially, they were given impetus by his work, as could be seen in the important books of the well-known pioneers which followed.[13] The change in designation of Rogers' contribution from nondirective to client-centered counseling indicated a transition from an emphasis on technique to the centrality of a particular quality of relationship, an observation that had already been made in the pastoral care and counseling field, but which was increasingly substantiated by Rogers' research data.[14] The training

[12] Richard C. Cabot and Russell L. Dicks, *The Arts of Ministering to the Sick* (New York: The Macmillan Co., 1936), pp. 189-203; Seward Hiltner, *Religion and Health* (New York: The Macmillan Co., 1943), pp. 167-205; Carl Rogers, *Counseling and Psychotherapy* (Boston: Houghton Mifflin, 1942).

[13] Russell Dicks, *Pastoral Work and Personal Counseling* (New York: The Macmillan Co., 1944); Seward Hiltner, *Pastoral Counseling* (New York: Abingdon Press, 1949); Paul E. Johnson, *Psychology of Pastoral Care* (Nashville: Abingdon Press, 1953); Oates, *The Christian Pastor*; Carroll A. Wise, *Pastoral Counseling: Theory and Practice* (New York: Harper & Row, 1951).

[14] Carl Rogers, *Client Centered Therapy* (Boston: Houghton Mifflin, 1951); *On Becoming a Person* (Boston: Houghton Mifflin, 1961).

29

of young ministers in the seminaries in this field was permeated by the client-centered understanding of the counseling relationship and process.

At times there intruded into this seminary scene some of the complex concepts of Freud, more frequently in the form of adding "depth" to the theoretical foundation of personality dynamics than in suggesting that the parish minister adapt psychoanalytic therapy to his counseling practice. Both Rogerian and Freudian therapy, however, seemed to assume that when the therapeutically oriented minister is confronted by a "serious" problem, he will need to arrange for a series of many weekly sessions with a person or persons before significant positive change can come about.

Short-Term Therapy

In recent years strong challenges have arisen both to the client-centered (as formerly understood) and psychoanalytic therapy, on theoretical and on practical levels, from sources that are really quite diverse. Even within psychoanalysis itself, practitioners have developed new techniques of short-term therapy.[15] On the whole, the trend has been toward greater personal involvement by the therapist and toward fewer sessions.

This is good news for the pastor for, on the one hand, his essential role is in the direction of active involvement with persons, and, on the other hand, this overly busy practitioner of the multiple functions that are demanded by the local church very rarely does any of the long-term therapy he has learned about in seminary.

[15] Leopold Bellak and Leonard Small, *Emergency Psychotherapy and Brief Psychotherapy* (New York: Grune & Stratton, 1965).

Even if he be quite well trained and emotionally prepared for a depth-counseling relationship of some
length, he simply does not often have the time for the
regular demands of it. Personal experience and discussion of counseling practices with many other ministers
has led me to the conclusion that the typical minister
sees very few persons for more than six hours in weekly
sessions. In one period of fifteen months as a pastoral
counseling specialist on the church staff, only fifteen out
of 154 different individuals, couples, or families who
came to me were seen for more than six sessions. Even
much contemporary psychiatric therapy confirms the effectiveness of brief contacts with most persons in need.
A well-known clinic in southern California has made a
study of 1097 patients who came to them for treatment
during a four-year period. Measurement in weeks of
contact shows that 37 percent of the patients were
helped and terminated within one week, 57 percent
within a month, and 79 percent within three months.
In the traditional training offered by most seminaries
in years past, the minister has not yet been clearly
shown how, in a reasonably brief period, he may help
effectively more persons who come to him with fairly
serious problems and toward whom he feels a pastoral
responsibility because of his own unique pastoral role.
This is not to discount the value of the minister as a
receptacle for the emotional catharsis of the temporarily
upset person, whose only need is to express his or her
emotions in the presence of an understanding listener
and whose emotional equilibrium is restored by only
one or two encounters. There continue to be a number
of these. Neither is this to discount the remarkable
contribution made to the personal lives and counseling

31

practice of many ministers by the type of training that the seminaries have offered in the past.

The Minister as a Mental Health Professional

However, within the past few years, a new approach to the resolution of many personal problems has been offered by some of the professionals working in the field of community psychiatry. More and more the inadequacy of traditional methods of long-term individual psychotherapy to deal with the constantly increasing mental health needs of our nation has become apparent. The facts are simple. In proportion to the total population and to the number of persons in need, there is a decreasing percentage of psychiatrists, clinical psychologists, and psychiatric social workers and nurses. There are at least two directions to go in search of an answer: new methods and new colaborers.

One large group of new colaborers, which this book proposes as at least a partial answer to the increasing mental health needs, is the clergy. They are already on the firing line. They live and work in all areas of the cities, small towns, and even the rural countryside. Many people already know them. Their presence is visible through the obvious presence of church buildings, in church services, and through their many community activities. A reasonably large number of people have some image of the minister as a person to turn to for help. Most ministers see themselves in the role of helper to all persons regardless of relationship to the church, education, race, social, or economic standing. They are usually available twenty-four hours a day and usually without financial cost to the person seeking help. A rather large number of them have at least a modest amount of training in various forms of helping. This number is rapidly increasing.

The Minister and Crisis Counseling

There is also a new method that is full of promise both for the traditional mental health professionals and for the minister. This is known as crisis intervention. For the pastor these techniques present a model for working with persons with problems—a model that seems to be more appropriate to his historic role, the types of problems he most frequently confronts, and the time available to him than those he probably studied in seminary, unless he graduated after the mid-1960s.

The term "crisis intervention," although it may carry a novel ring, when pondered for a moment, is not at all a surprising one to apply to the work of the minister, who is continually intervening in some crisis, and who does so both by invitation and by his own initiative. It is no more than stepping into a disturbed situation or the life of a disturbed person at an opportune time in such a way as to stop the downward spiral of a deteriorating situation or condition and to bring love, support, assurance, and insight in an effort to lead to decisions that can redirect life. Every minister has already been doing this in critical illness, serious accident, a major move or vocational change, family disruption, dying, suicide, grief, intense emotional distress and its accompanying behavioral changes.

Now, however, as a result of the systematic work of several groups of mental health practitioners, a clear model of operating procedure is being offered to the minister for his testing, adaptation, use, and perhaps modification. It is the theory and methodology of crisis intervention, particularly as it relates to the work of the clergyman, and especially the parish minister, that this book will seek to examine and elaborate. First, crisis theory as such will be discussed, for the theory is directly tied to practice. Next, the details of crisis intervention will be presented in the context of important understandings of the necessary ingredients for all effective counseling. The major portion of the rest of the book will look at specific situations of crisis and how the minister may appropriately and helpfully function in these situations.

The grief situation has been selected for detailed examination for several reasons. First, it was through systematic observations of grief reactions that contemporary crisis theory was given its initial impetus in psychiatry, and it remains something of the prototype of crisis. Second, it is a situation in which the minister is constantly and frequently called upon to function in a helping way and in which his effectiveness is often crucial for the later well-being of the persons involved. Finally, it provides an opportunity to present a model of the methodology of active crisis counseling (see chapter 6).

Crises arising in the context of marriage and family life are included because of their prevalence in our society and the frequency with which the minister is involved. This, along with grief, would comprise a high percentage of the counseling work of most clergy. Just as it is important to understand the dynamics of the individual in crisis, so is it necessary to understand the dynamics of the family system to appreciate the origin and process of the family crisis. One major crisis of the family that has received all too little attention as far as an understanding of its emotional aftermath is concerned is that of divorce. It seems appropriate to stress this for the minister.

A rationale might be made for the inclusion of a discussion of the suicidal crisis and the minister's role in working with the suicidal person and the family in which there has been a suicide. Certainly suicide and its aftermath is a serious problem in our country. It is the number ten cause of death, and number five among adolescents and young adults fifteen to twenty-four years of age. These figures should not be misinterpreted however, since the actual rate of suicide tends to increase with age.[16] The rate of reported suicide has increased between 1956-57 and 1966-67 for both sexes, both white and nonwhite, in all age categories, except for very slight declines for white males forty-five to sixty-four years of age and nonwhite males sixty-five and over, and about a 20 percent decline for white males sixty-five and over. There has been an especially rapid increase among females under sixty-five.[17] It is estimated that there are approximately fifteen attempts for every successful suicide.[18] Nevertheless, studies indicate that in total numbers most ministers have relatively little contact with highly lethal persons and few opportunities to work with the families of persons who have committed suicide, 50 percent indicating no counseling contact at all with suicidal persons.[19] These contacts

[16] Paul W. Pretzel, *Understanding and Counseling the Suicidal Person* (Nashville: Abingdon Press, 1972), pp. 20, 62, 66.

[17] "Suicide-International Comparisons," *Statistical Bulletin of Metropolitan Life Insurance Co.*, LIII (August, 1972), p. 2.

[18] Pretzel, *Understanding and Counseling*, p. 20.

[19] Doman Lum, "Suicide: Theological Ethics and Pastoral Counseling" (Ph.D. dissertation, School of Theology at Claremont, Calif., 1967).

may increase, along with both the rising rate and the minister's greater activity and competence in many areas of human need. There is no question as to the high priority for the minister's work with suicidal people. The major reason for not preparing a chapter on intervention in the suicidal crisis is the recent appearance of Pretzel's book which gives a superb understanding of the suicidal person as well as complete and clear guidelines for the minister's functioning. It would only be superfluous to seek to present similar material here. Those interested in pursuing this topic should turn to this excellent work.

Finally, the important issue of the minister and his relationship to those community agencies and resources appropriate to his work in the various crisis areas will be discussed, along with the significance of his own constant context, the community of faith. It is hoped that this book will enable the minister to function with increased competence with persons in distress, not as a "baptized" traditional psychotherapist, but in ways consistent with his vocational identity as a minister, utilizing perhaps some new concepts and methodologies and certainly learning from new research, but combining these with his uniqueness as a *pastoral* counselor in potently healing ways.

To state the purpose of the book in these terms is neither to overlook nor depreciate the highly significant point made by Jernigan that "pastoral care, as the total ministry of the religious community to individuals and families in crisis, should include both ministries of healing and comfort and ministries of preparation." [20] He

---

[20] Homer L. Jernigan, "Pastoral Care and the Crises of Life," in *Community Mental Health: The Role of Church and Temple*, Howard Clinebell, Jr., ed., (Nashville: Abingdon Press, 1970), p. 57.

goes on to indicate that pastoral care oriented exclusively or primarily toward pathology or evident situational trouble spots is a quite inadequate response to the larger and long-range goals of the church in relation to the total needs of individuals, families, the congregation, and the larger community.[21] There is no question in my mind that he has thrown out the challenge for the development of a comprehensive church program and quality of congregational life and activity that has implications reaching farther than the major emphasis of this particular book. However, day by day ministers and members of congregations continue to be confronted by the hurt, distress, panic, and sense of hopelessness that persons and families experience when a crisis is actually upon them. There continues then to be the need to understand and work effectively with these persons. To increase such understanding and to facilitate such work is the limited, but still important intent of these pages.

[21] *Ibid.*, p. 59.

Chapter II

CRISIS THEORY: DEFINITION, DESCRIPTION, DYNAMICS

Case # 1

Mr. Jones slammed on the brakes but not in time to avoid hitting the boy who had dashed out in the street in front of his car. Before he could even open the door of the car, he felt nauseated and very frightened. He managed, almost blindly, to reach the front of the car but found himself unable to do anything to assist the moaning teen-ager who was badly cut and bleeding. When help arrived, Mr. Jones was in a dazed condition, unable to talk coherently about the accident but aware that he was tremendously disturbed. Fortunately, the boy's injuries seemed much more severe than they actually were, and he recovered with no permanent injuries. Although Mr. Jones was found not to be legally responsible for the accident—and the boy whom he hit fully admitted that it was not Mr. Jones' fault—it was months before Mr. Jones was able to talk about the accident and drive his car comfortably.

Case # 2

Mr. Jones's peculiar behavior had begun very gradually. At first he seemed to become forgetful, then simply "off on another planet" most of the time. When Mrs. Jones would try to call it to his attention, she found him completely unaware of his actions. Then one day he just disappeared. There was simply no trace of him for nearly a week, when he was found by a United States Customs officer returning to New York on a flight from Europe. He was arguing with the officer about paying duty on a guitar he had bought in Spain, and he had attracted quite a crowd. He was very belligerent and the officer, suspecting he was not well, called the police—who in turn called an ambulance. In the ambulance Mr. Jones suddenly seemed to realize who and where he was and, after satisfying the medical authorities that he was well, was released. He was home again the next day, virtually back to normal.[1]

Does either of the above stories portray a person in crisis? If so, which one? Or do both of them? How does one make such a determination? Does it matter?

The clear preference for many people in most situations is definitely not to get bogged down in the detail of theoretical considerations. The practical matters are what count. However, it is of some real importance to get clearly in mind what the state of crisis is, primarily because, as self-evident as it may sound, the methodology of crisis intervention does not work very well unless the person needing help is actually in a crisis. The how-to is tightly tied to the theory. Therefore, the minister must be able to identify the characteristics of crisis and understand what the person is experiencing in order, first, to make the decision to utilize the methodology, and second, to function effectively.

THE DEVELOPMENT OF CRISIS THEORY

It is ironic that the major impetus to the development of contemporary crisis theory and modes of inter-

[1] Bernard Bloom, "Definitional Aspects of the Crisis Concept," *Journal of Consulting Psychology*, XXVII (1963), 499.

vention being proposed to the minister as a means of upgrading the quality of his counseling practice actually grew out of a psychiatrist's involvement in an area of human distress that is usually the domain of the minister himself, namely, grief. Numerous writers have recounted the events first reported by Dr. Erich Lindemann in an article in 1944.[2] Very briefly, survivors of the disastrous Cocoanut Grove nightclub fire of 1942, in which over 490 persons finally died, were taken to Massachusetts General Hospital, where Dr. Lindemann began to notice certain characteristic responses on the part of those who had lost close relatives in the fire. These were the familiar symptoms of grief, which show the behavior of personality decompensation in response to the loss of an emotionally significant person. Both realistic and unrealistic methods of coping with this loss were called up, and where realistic methods were ineffective, unrealistic defenses and methods of escape and denial took over. When these unrealistic mechanisms were dealt with by the psychiatrist's facilitating the person's grief work—i.e., in relationship with the grief sufferer helping him test reality with its pain and find new patterns of rewarding interaction—the person once again established himself and reentered life with new resources for dealing with crisis. Again, in all this, there is nothing particularly new for the sensitive and faithful minister, but it was systematized so that further psychiatric investigation of crisis could be made.

Religious Origins

It is also ironic that the concept of crisis was not more familiar to ministers as well as to psychiatrists prior to

[2] Erich Lindemann, "Symptomatology and Management of Acute Grief," *Pastoral Psychology*, XIV (September, 1963), 8-18.

that time, since material was already available in the work of Anton Boisen. As early as 1923 he published his evolving ideas based on his own experience and on his observations, which were to be presented in their more developed form later. Essentially he recognized the increasing tension of inner conflicts, which were neither good nor bad in and of themselves, but which comprised an intermediate stage that a person must pass through in order to reach a higher level of development. The higher level meant a reintegration of the individual's personality, bringing greater insight, new perspectives, and additional strength. However, there were dangers, and if the reintegration did not take place the result was decompensation, the moods and behavior of mental illness.[3] Still without using the word "crisis," Boisen developed these ideas in detail in his classic and provocative book, *The Exploration of the Inner World,* in 1936. Here, in the context of the examination of the relationship between religious experience and psychosis, he reiterated the make-or-break nature of a high level of anxiety, to the point of panic.[4] There were always possibilities in the conflict, because old and inadequate methods of coping were challenged and barriers to growth were removed.[5] Even when there was breakdown to the point of psychosis, it could be viewed as a problem-solving possibility, as a person sought "to assimilate hitherto unassimilated masses of life experience."[6] The outcome, Boisen felt, was dependent "upon the presence or absence of an acceptable nucleus

[3] Anton Boisen, "Concerning the Relationship between Religious Experience and Mental Disorders," *Mental Hygiene,* VII (April 1923), 308-9.
[4] Anton Boisen, *The Exploration of the Inner World* (New York: Harper & Brothers, 1936), p. 54.
[5] *Ibid.,* p. 46.
[6] *Ibid.,* p. 54.

of purpose around which the new self can be formed." [7]

The most complete presentation of his theory of crisis came in 1945 with the publication of *Religion in Crisis and Custom*, partially based on papers published during the late 1930s. Here he outlines three categories: normal developmental crises, situational frustration, and intrapsychic conflict.

The developmental crises are those we would expect: adolescence, marriage, birth of children, aging, bereavement, death. There are the heightened emotions of any crisis period, the need for readjustment, the attempt to find meaning, the potential for positive and negative outcome. [8]

Situational crises are reactions to the serious frustrations produced by specific external events, such as marriage disruption, business or job failure. Frustration is a condition of growth, and the way a person handles and assimilates these is determinative of his direction in life. [9]

Finally, Boisen takes into consideration personality aspects of individuals that form barriers to effective dealing with stressful events. [10] This is not precisely what his outline would have led us to believe, in that the crisis is not caused by "intrapsychic conflict," but Boisen is correct in introducing those factors that make persons particularly vulnerable to stress and limit their appropriate and constructive responses.

Crisis is characterized by anxiety, self-blame, and frequently a sense of personal failure and guilt, which

[7] *Ibid.*, p. 56
[8] Anton Boisen, *Religion in Crisis and Custom* (New York: Harper & Brothers, 1955), pp. 42-43.
[9] *Ibid.*, pp. 43-44.
[10] *Ibid.*, pp. 44-45.

lead to a constricted perspective on accumulating problems. There is the combination of tremendous emotional impact along with a diminishing ability to see the problems clearly and deal with them. There is, of course, danger to the person, and it may be a shattering experience. However, because there is also a speeding up of the emotional and intellectual processes, there is the potential for new insights, and therefore not only a solution of the problems but also a reorganization of personality around a new center and on a higher level. At this point, Boisen appropriately introduces religious experience as one form that the crisis and its resolution may take.[11]

It is clear that while Boisen has made a unique contribution, there are elements of his theory of crisis and their relationship both to personality decompensation and to religious experience that have their roots in the studies of James, Starbuck, and others around the turn of the century.[12]

Psychiatric Origins

The major figure in the systematic development of crisis theory within psychiatry was Gerald Caplan, who, with Lindemann, established a community mental health program in the Cambridge, Massachusetts area in 1946. Much of what has been done in this field during the last decade has been an elaboration of, or at least somehow in response to, Caplan's work.[13] A crisis, according to Caplan, arises out of some change in a

---

[11] *Ibid.*, pp. 67-69, 3-4.

[12] William James, *The Varieties of Religious Experience* (New York: Longmans, Green and Co., 1902); Edwin Starbuck, *Psychology of Religion* (New York: Charles Scribner's Sons, 1900).

[13] Gerald Caplan, *Principles of Preventive Psychiatry* (New York: Basic Books, 1964).

person's life space that produces a modification of his relationship with others and/or his perceptions of himself. Such a change may come about relatively slowly and as a result of rather normal and inevitable experiences of growing and developing physically and socially or quite rapidly as a result of some unforeseen and traumatic event. These two concepts have been differentiated by referring to them as developmental and accidental crises.

Erikson has elaborated the former in detail. He proposes that life is to be thought of as a series of stages, eight of them, each one of which has significance in and of itself, but each also contributes to or detracts from the achievement of the goal of "integrity," as he has designated the positive goal of the final stage. Each of these stages has its task and outcome characterized by contrasting terms, one emphasizing the positive need and the positive outcome, if the need is successfully met, and the other a possible negative result. For example, the series of stages of childhood are basic trust versus mistrust, autonomy versus shame and doubt, initiative versus guilt, and industry versus inferiority. The needs and conflicts of adolescence are penetratingly and helpfully elaborated in the discussion of identity versus self-diffusion. Adulthood consists progressively of intimacy versus self-absorption, generativity versus stagnation, and finally, integrity versus despair. It is made clear that if a person is to accomplish the tasks and have the needs of one of these stages adequately met, it is important that basic trust has been established in the very first stage, and that the outcome of each successive stage be more on the positive side than on the negative. Each of these stages is a developmental crisis because each is both the opportunity for significant growth and an occasion for the dangers of the failure to grow. Each has its own particular emotional stress. So long as a person stays alive, there is no possibility of avoiding having to deal with the external and internal situations presented by each stage.[14] While the developmental crises are significant periods in a person's life, and each has implications for the total ministry of the church (sacrament and ritual; fellowship, growth, and study groups; personal and group counseling), it is not the purpose of this book to seek to deal with them.

THE SITUATIONAL CRISIS: DESCRIPTION AND DYNAMICS

An accidental, or situational, crisis differs primarily in the matters of the source of stress and the element of time. There is a more rapid modification of a person's perception of himself and his world, including frequently relationships with other persons, usually initiated by some type of personal loss that is perceived as a threat to the self. Along with this form of external event, or in place of it, there may be some other sudden change in a situation that challenges one's self-concept or sense of identity. In either case, there is the self-perception of being threatened, with movement in the direction of feeling one's self unable to cope with the situation with the usual repertoire of behavioral responses at one's disposal.

Thus, according to Rapoport, "There are three sets of interrelated factors that can produce a state of

[14] Erik Erikson, "Growth and Crises of the 'Healthy Personality.'" in *Personality in Nature, Society, and Culture,* Clyde Kluckhohn and Henry A. Murray, eds. (New York: Alfred A. Knopf, 1956), pp. 185-225.

crisis: (1) a hazardous event which poses some threat; (2) a threat to instinctual need which is symbolically linked to earlier threats that resulted in vulnerability or conflict; (3) an inability to respond with adequate coping mechanisms." [15]

The threat-producing event, in other words, has the power, because of its similarity in some ways to prior events in our lives, to arouse earlier feelings of anxiety that have been repressed or covered over in some way. Therefore, in the present we have a sense of a double fear operating, having sufficient cumulative power to make us feel highly vulnerable. An inevitable part of this experience of increasing vulnerability is the individual's perception of himself as being less and less capable of coping with this event and the feelings that have been aroused. The crisis, then, is not necessarily inherent in the external situation itself. To be sure, there are certain events involving serious personal loss that we may predict with some high degree of reliability will produce the response of crisis in most people. However, it should be made clear that the crisis itself is the internal reaction to the external event, and events that may be very threatening for some may not be for others.

In crisis theory there is the assumption that there are a number of physical, psychosocial, and sociocultural needs that contribute to the fundamental ego integrity of a person. The physical needs are rather obvious. Among the most important psychosocial needs are those that cluster around the person's relationship with others within his family and with those outside the family, so that his cognitive and emotional development are

[15] Lydia Rapoport, "The State of Crisis: Some Theoretical Considerations," in *Crisis Intervention: Selected Readings*, Howard J. Parad, ed. (New York: Family Service Association of America, 1965), pp. 25-26.

46

stimulated, his needs for love and affection met, behavioral guidelines are given, personal support is supplied, reality-testing takes place, and the opportunities are provided to work with others on tasks seen to be significant. The sociocultural supplies include the influence of the customs and values of society on personal development and behavior. These help locate the person's position in the social order and afford an external structure and an inner security as the context for living out one's life. The sudden shutting off of one or more of these supplies cues off a perception of threat to one's basic integrity as a person. This is a crisis, which produces a series of adaptational struggles in order to preserve one's identity.[16]

For example, physical illness often produces crisis. Two factors seem to be involved. One is the relationship between the concept of body image and the whole self. The first major step in the development of the self is the infant's finally coming to the place where he can distinguish between what is outside of his skin and what is inside, the delineation of his own body, the setting it off from the rest of the world. The full psychosocial self of the adult is preceded in time by the recognition of the physical self, and therefore the body image forms the foundation of and is incorporated into what later comes to be the total self. Thus, any change in or attack upon the body is perceived to be an attack upon one's whole being. The observable physical changes of early adolescence are first experienced as a changing of the self, and call for readjustment. The same is true of other stages of the aging process, and of illness, surgery, or accident. The perception of this threat is experienced as anxiety, and in the case of the

[16] Caplan, *Principles of Preventive Psychiatry*, pp. 31-33.

medical patient, it is not always proportionate to the medically diagnosed seriousness of the disorder.

A second factor involved is that in the face of this anxiety there is often the beginning of the breakdown of one's personal world. This means the breakdown of that pattern of meaningful relationships in which we exist and by which we live. The patient who is already experiencing threat to his self as anxiety, if hospitalized, is now taken out of his familiar and somewhat secure context of living and thrust into a new and strange situation and is relatively isolated. Opportunities for reality-testing are minimized, and so a sense of peril and ideas of self-reference have more fertile soil in which to grow. There may be the beginning of the loss of identity, and personal identity is always based upon and is in relation to community. This was true developmentally and continues to be true in terms of the relationship of internal dynamics and external social situations throughout life. We come to know who we are because of the communities in which we were born and raised, and frequently in illness we feel separated from those communities that sustain us as persons.

So the physical illness or other attack upon the body in and of itself is perceived as a threat to the self; but further, there is the loss to some degree of previously meaningful extensions of one's self, those objects and persons in the external world with which we have identified, that is, taken into ourselves as a part of our personal identity. In this situation there are heightened demands on the individual without an increase of psychosocial supplies. To the contrary, there may be the withdrawal of these supplies. So in addition to the double sense of threat, there is the appraisal of one's self in the situation as having reduced resources with which to cope with one's feelings. Understanding this, the minister can see with perhaps greater clarity than before the overarching importance of visiting the sick and particularly those who are in the hospital as the result of illness or surgery or accident. He not only provides the opportunity for the patient to express his feelings, reduce the pressure of them, and objectify them, but he also gives an increased sense of personal support and the support of the community of faith and the faith itself.

Other situations frequently productive of crisis in somewhat similar terms are the death of an emotionally significant person, change in or loss of job, disruption of a family, change of role due to developmental or cultural transitions. One study of 108 patients who came into a mental health clinic during a period of a year and a half shows the following most frequent "hazardous situations": loss of a family member, the disturbed behavior of a family member, a new family member, moving, the change of role within or outside of marriage, and the isolation of a family from the community. Often there was an additional force which led the person to seek help after he or she was already beginning to be aware of rising anxiety, such as a talk with a friend, a minister, or a doctor. The anxiety felt was the main motivating force, and the desire for relief the primary goal.[17] The observations are quite close to the experiences of most ministers.

Another study made an intensive examination of the precipitating stress that led forty persons to seek treatment in a psychiatric clinic. The purpose was to organize the variety of stresses into descriptive

[17] Peter E. Sifneos, "A Concept of 'Emotional Crisis,'" *Mental Hygiene*, XLIV (April 1960), 169-71.

categories.[18] All but one of these are relevant to the onset of crisis. The following are the important broad categories to keep in mind.

The first, already clearly referred to, is object loss or the threat of loss.

The second is frustration with a previous source of help. One would presume here that there had been a need of some kind, not a crisis, for which assistance was sought from some person or agency, but for some reason help in the expected form was not forthcoming. At least in some instances, this disappointing result would arouse emotions that the person could not express appropriately and effectively and that he now felt incapable of handling. Or there may have been produced a sense of hopelessness and helplessness that the person had not experienced before.

The third form of precipitating stress is a product of a person's identification with someone else. When this other person becomes involved in a situation similar to that in the first person's own past, then the original conflict and painful emotions are aroused to an intense degree. There is not always the awareness of what is taking place or why, and a cry for help is forthcoming. For example, a middle-aged woman may at one time in her life have experienced a very painful divorce with anger, bitterness, guilt, yet a sense of loss. With remarriage and the passing of the years, those feelings have become deeply submerged and are never consciously felt and seldom thought of. Now, however, her own daughter is going through a divorce, and she herself is having a severe emotional reaction to it, with

[18] Betty L. Kalis, M. Robert Harris, A. Rodney Prestwood, and Edith H. Freeman, "Precipitating Stress as a Focus in Psychotherapy," *Archives of General Psychiatry*, V (September, 1961), 221-24.

feelings of depression, anger at her daughter, feelings of guilt toward her present husband, and she is quite surprised at her inability to handle her feelings.

A fourth category of precipitating stress is any event that produces a threat to one's present level of adjustment. A person is confronted with a decision, perhaps one which on the surface would seem to hold positive promise, but which would still require leaving his present psychological equilibrium. There may be attraction and threat at the same time. A man may not only be threatened in this way by the loss of a job or a demotion, but may be also thrown into a state of anxiety and immobility by the offer of a promotion.

Life is to be viewed as a continual series of new experiences, and therefore of demands upon the organism to cope with the internal pressure brought about by one's own maturational processes or by the external stimuli of a continually changing environment. Most of these do not place excessive demands upon an individual, because his past learning includes a repertoire of adaptive responses that have been interpersonally and intrapsychically effective in maintaining a relatively homeostatic condition. (*Homeostasis* refers simply to a relative balance of internal forces with one another, and can be extended even to mean a relative balance between internal and external demands.) The similarity of the external occasion for the present anxiety to earlier occasions and the knowledge of one's own problem-solving resources lead to an evaluation which includes the expectation of a successful resolution. However, when the novelty of the situation is such or the personal loss is perceived as being so great that these usual methods of coping do not seem to be appropriate or strong enough, there is a severe disruption of the usual emotional life which may be compared to the disruption caused by a normal maturational transition. Every developmental state or major life decision, as we have seen, has its stresses: the anxiety of giving up old patterns of responding, the threat of new responsibilities and situations calling for new forms of coping, new relationships with persons, and new relationships between meanings, as well as the creating of new meanings. An accidental crisis is a problem situation that places these same demands upon the individual, but is compressed into a brief period of time. Major alterations in pattern may occur rather rapidly, yet may subsequently persist as new aspects of personality.[19] It is important to note that the determining factor is not just the difficulty of the situation as such, but its importance to the person, the degree of ego involvement, the amount of threat felt, and the way the person perceives the resources available to him to remove the threat in the learned, expected period of time. This brief transitional period has the power, due to its emotional intensity, to produce significant personality change. Clinical evidence points to the first six weeks as being vital in giving the direction.[20] This personality change can be positive or negative, adding to or taking strength away from one's ego, depending upon whether new and effective means of coping have been developed or whether there has been behavioral decompensation.

Caplan has outlined four phases of the crisis situation which give a picture of the process taking place:

1. There is the original rise in tension from the problem stimulus, the experience of anxiety, perceived threat

[19] Caplan, *Principles of Preventive Psychiatry*, p. 39.
[20] Wilbur E. Morley, "Treatment of the Patient in Crisis," *Western Medicine*, III (March, 1965).

to the self. This calls forth the habitual problem-solving responses which have been learned previously and which might be generalized to this particular problem stimulus.

2. Because of the novelty of the situation and the continuing intensity of the stimulus, there is a lack of success in reducing the anxiety with the usual coping mechanisms in the period of time expected. A feeling of helplessness and ineffectualness results.

3. This is the "hitching up the belt" stage. The person dips deep into his reserve of strength and extends the range of his behavior in attempting to maintain his ego integrity. A redefinition of the problem may bring it into the range of prior experience. Trial and error behavior, both in thinking and in overt act, seeks to change or remove the problem stimulus. There may be a redefinition of one's role, thus a modification of identity. Active resignation may be integrated into the self image. The problem may be solved in this phase. If it is, the person usually becomes stronger, he moves farther along the continuum toward mental health, in that he has learned methods of dealing effectively with a new and threatening situation and has now brought this new learning into his repertoire of responses.

4. However, if the problem continues with no need satisfaction, the tension produced by the anxiety may take the person beyond the threshold of rational responding, described by the term personality decompensation, where there are exaggerated distortions of one's identity or of the situation, rigid and compulsive and ineffective behavior, socially unacceptable behavior, extreme withdrawal, *et cetera*.[21]

It can be observed that one of the characteristics of crisis, as well as a factor that has the effect of intensifying

[21] Caplan, *Principles of Preventive Psychiatry*, pp. 40-41.

it, is the narrowing of the usual range of attention, with more and more focus being on the anguish of the condition, emphasizing only a few of the features of the total situation to the exclusion of others, thus causing a greater sense of one's inadequacy and of the hopelessness of it all.

During the last decade of increased interest in the development of an understanding of crisis and the attempt to develop effective forms of intervention, numerous therapists and other investigators have sought to define and describe it. Some of the results have been somewhat less than useful in clarifying the matter, primarily as a result of some differences in concept and practical evaluation on the part of therapists themselves. It would seem from the point of view of the minister's own practice, the need to determine whether the reaction of a specific person is a crisis or not, with the obvious implications for the counseling methodology with this person, can be met by answering three questions: (1) Has there been a recent (within a few weeks) onset of the troublesome feelings and/or behavior? (2) Have they tended to grow progressively worse? (3) Can the time of onset be linked with some external event, some change in the person's life situation?

Taplin has made an important contribution by viewing the concept of crisis in terms of a perceptual and cognitive disorder. He points out that observations of persons in crisis indicate that a breakdown of thinking begins to take place under a physical or psychological overload, where there is an input of information that is significantly incompatible with one's present pattern of thinking about himself, his world, his relationships. This inevitably means that the dissonant information interferes with one's usual forms of planning and carrying out effective behavior. Crisis, then, is defined in terms of a cognitive perspective that can include all the presently observed behavior involved in the condition (an identifiable, disorienting perception; a sudden decrease in memory recall and in planning ability; an increase in aimless behavior, emotionality, suggestibility). This conceptuality also provides an accounting for therapeutic procedures which themselves are primarily cognitive in nature: direct teaching of information-processing techniques, the giving of information itself, leading to a more realistic appraisal of one's self and one's world, and the making of appropriate decisions issuing in constructive behavior.[22]

After this is said, however, the issue of greatest importance to ministers and to lay workers in helping situations is not the specific technical theory of personality to which they adhere, but whether they are able to identify a crisis, to distinguish it from disorders related to longer-standing pathology, to understand the dynamics of personality in this particular situation, and to function effectively in reducing the intensity of emotion and helping a person to new perspectives about himself and his situation and to effective decision-making.

The implication throughout this discussion of the nature of the crisis is that the power of the intense emotion and the state where earlier patterns of structured behavior have broken down combine to produce a situation in which a person may either go under or may experience rapid new growth. One writer has expressed another aspect of the total human picture by saying that "continual gratification of stability does not seem

[22] Julian R. Taplin, "Crisis Theory: Critique and Reformulation," *Community Mental Health Journal*, VII (March, 1971), 13-23.

conducive to rapid change or growth." [23] The very nature of crisis is that it forces change and readjustment. A person must learn new methods of coping that become a part of increased adaptability, resiliency, and strength. "At crisis a painfully unstable state of psychological affairs exists and some kind of equilibrium must be established for a person to become oriented effectively to the future. . . . [Therefore it] represents both a need and an opportunity for significant growth and creativity and lowers resistance to utilizing interpersonal experience and other kinds of information in new ways, to seeking newly conceived experiences or accepting formerly rejected ones." [24]

An extremely important factor to keep in mind is that a person usually does not face a crisis alone, and therefore he is either helped or hindered in his task of maintaining himself as a person by the other significant persons about him: family, friends, coworkers, members of the groups to which he belongs, professional workers of various kinds, of which the minister is an important figure for many people. Are these persons involved in the sufferer's life in such a way as to be giving psychosocial need satisfactions that compensate for the need frustration in other areas? Does the minister, for example, visit in the hospital? Does he come by and continue to see people in grief? Does he work with the family of one who has been hospitalized with an emotional disorder? Do the minister and other significant persons offer the opportunity for new decisions, new behavioral forms, new roles that are ego-strengthening?

During a crisis a person is more open to influence by

[23] Bertram R. Forer, "The Therapeutic Value of Crisis," *Psychological Reports*, XIII (1963), 276.
[24] *Ibid.*, p. 277.

others than he is at any other time. His emotional equilibrium is upset, his thinking is unclear, and even a relatively minor force will be able to tip him to the side of resolution of the problem and additional strength or toward failure and increased vulnerability and potential decompensation of behavior. The presence of significant other persons may have a major effect in determining the choice of coping mechanisms, which in turn influence the outcome of the crisis.[25] It is at this point that a discussion of the role of the minister and the methodology of crisis counseling properly arise for discussion.

[25] Caplan, *Principles of Preventive Psychiatry*, p. 48.

Chapter III

METHODS OF CRISIS COUNSELING

In a comprehensive overview of the methods of crisis counseling it is necessary to talk about much more than methods as such and in the narrow sense of the word. Purpose, persons, and process are tied inseparably together. These, along with their corollaries, can be discussed independently of one another, although never without obvious overlap. This is the way it must be in terms of the practicalities of presentation. Nevertheless, it should be understood at every point that these elements are a part of the unified whole of what crisis counseling is all about. This chapter, then, is to be an examination of the five elements which comprise this whole:

1. The goal of crisis counseling
2. The role of words in the interaction
3. The person of the helper himself
4. The basic conditions necessary for counselee improvement in any counseling
5. The process and methods of crisis counseling

GOAL

The goal of *crisis* counseling can be stated very simply, and needs only a little elaboration. Very concisely, it is the quickest possible relief of the internal and external symptoms of the crisis and a return to that particular person's usual level of functioning. In actual practice it is recognized that many crises will leave their residue of hurt and therefore residual feelings and occasional behavioral responses to these. In this sense, it is unrealistic to expect a person to be precisely the same as before. Also, in many instances of the successful resolution of crisis new learning will have taken place; new methods of coping as a by-product of the resolution process will be added to one's repertoire of behavior designed to deal with stress and loss. So in an additional sense, the person is not the same, and in reality is functioning at an improved level. Therefore, it is appropriate to consider some real growth as a reasonable expectation of working directly toward crisis resolution.

The tricky part of defining this goal of symptom relief for any given person is that the feelings and behavior of crisis must be distinguished from the feelings and behavior of the person's precrisis condition. Not only are the methods of crisis intervention inappropriate where there is a chronic pathological condition without crisis, but it must also be understood that a person with a chronic disturbance may also suffer a crisis. In that person a differentiation between the symptoms must be made, with the crisis counseling to be directed only at the behavior of the crisis. The attempt to deal with the prior condition at the same time and with the same methods must not be made. A specific case to be presented later will seek to illustrate this point as well as to demonstrate the basic methods of crisis intervention.

However, in such instances, it is possible that the effectiveness of the minister as he works with a person in crisis may in itself provide the stimulus to motivate the person to seek additional help with other problems.

In summary, the single goal of crisis counseling contains inherently within it a series of expectations:

1. Symptom relief: the alleviation of immediate distress, the cessation of the maladaptive behavior of the crisis
2. Actual growth through the learning of new coping methods
3. The continuance in counseling with the same or another person when there are other problems yet to be resolved

THE ROLE OF WORDS
IN THE INTERACTION

It is somewhat amazing to many people at first brief consideration to realize that a relationship and a process as potent as that of counseling and psychotherapy takes place chiefly through an exchange of words. Of course, as far as the minister is concerned, something of the same thing could be said for preaching. Therefore, it is imperative that we look more deeply at the meaning of the spoken word from one person to another. When we do so, we discover that a word is never *merely* a word. It is an *act* of the whole person like any other act. It becomes then a form of delivering ourselves to another person. It is a reflection of who we are, an acting out of our being in relation to another being.

In order to grasp fully this level of meaning of spoken words, an elaboration of the development of personality and the role of the learning and the use of language in the early development of the child would be necessary. Such a detailed elaboration is beyond the scope of this book, and, in fact, is to be found in an earlier work.[1] Only the very briefest summary will be presented here.

Talking is originally learned by every child in the context of the emotionally charged relationship of absolute dependence upon the parents. The original meaning of talking then gains its full force from this relationship. It is learned in a very complex process combining the beginning natural expression of sounds on the part of the child, the imitation of that which the parents are seeking to teach by a method of rewarding certain sounds over certain other sounds, and by actual identification with the behavior of the parent. This last factor means that the language of the parent and the attitudes that the parent has toward the child are incorporated by the child as a part of his own self. Language then is literally an integral part of one's self. Talking is practiced by the child first, as a necessary means of communicating basic survival and comfort needs, second, as a means of winning and maintaining parental approval, and third, as a means of holding the parents emotionally near even when the child is alone. In all three of these ways, talking is a means of anxiety reduction, a learned method of overcoming separation. Language continues to have something of this affective and relational meaning throughout a person's life. It is important to keep this in mind as the relationship and process of crisis counseling are discussed.

In this context it is easy to see that there is a unity of language and personality. Talking is one of the most

[1] David K. Switzer, *The Dynamics of Grief* (Nashville: Abingdon Press, 1970), pp. 79-91.

important ways that we have of establishing meaningful relationships, reducing anxiety, and communicating meaning, emotional as well as intellectual. In human life one act may substitute for another. This is not to say that they are identical in meaning, potency, and effect, but depending upon the quality of the act, its context, and a number of other factors, it moves more or less in the direction of being the same. Talking is an act that is frequently a substitute for other acts. For example, we talk angrily or sarcastically or in a demeaning manner instead of hitting another person. This then is the power of spoken word in counseling. It is emotional-relational in its very nature, and it encompasses all the time dimensions.

Something of the meaning of talking in counseling as it relates to the time dimensions may be shown in the following diagram:

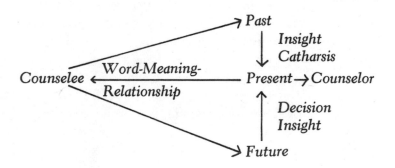

The word is *in* the present, and, in fact, in the moment of counseling, *is* the present. It is in the context of a personal, affective relationship, and it is the means of developing and maintaining that relationship, a security measure, and an ego-fulfilling act.

But the present word frequently refers to the past,

either near or distant. The counselee reaches back into his past, has an image of that which took place, speaks the present word describing the past, and therefore in effect by telling his story presents a contemporary re-enactment of the past: its relationships, acts, feelings. His words are present acts substituting for past acts, and within the reenactment they have the potential for clarifying the past, bringing insight into the present, and producing catharsis, the pressure relieving expression of emotion.

By the same token the present word may move and indeed *must* move into the future in order to bring it into the present for testing. Again, we have a present act, substituting this time for a future one, testing future action in the present to try to determine what it *will be* like, but without all the consequences. Therefore, it too has the power to bring insight into the present, and leads to decision-making on the basis of the present testing of the future. Counseling is this kind of present, past-present, and future-present relationship, established and expedited by the use of spoken words.

THE PERSON OF THE COUNSELOR

Carkhuff points out that there are four factors that interact to affect the outcome of any counseling: the person needing help, the counselor, the setting of the counseling relationship and process and the total context that develops out of the relationship and process, and the daily environment of the person in distress (home and family, work, friends, group membership).[2]

---

[2] Carkhuff, *Helping and Human Relations*, Vol. I, pp. 33-74.

In regard to the person needing help, the identifiable common characteristics of crisis have already been discussed, as has the fact that the precrisis condition will differ from person to person. The influence of one's total physical environment, the quality of the behavior of family, friends, and coworkers in relation to the person in crisis, and the number and degree of meaningfulness of his or her activities, including work, would seem to be rather obvious. The relationship between the counselor and the person needing help and what that produces will be discussed later. Not the least of these factors in potency is the helper himself.

It was stated in chapter 2 that in the midst of the transition, the unsettled thought and the disturbed emotions of a person in crisis, intervention by another person has a potential for tremendous influence. One would naturally expect that those with the most influence would be the persons who are already linked to the one in crisis by bonds of love and who play a role in his or her particular pattern of needs. Caplan confirms this judgment.[3] The closer one is to the needs of the sufferer, the closer he actually is to the crisis, the more likely he is to be called on, and the easier it usually is for him to intervene at his own initiative.

Few persons are in more strategic position for intervention in crisis in terms of visibility, availability, and previously established relationships than the alert and sensitive minister. Caplan himself notes this and makes a point of particular value to us in the ministry who sometimes feel a bit unsure of ourselves as we move into the role of psychotherapists. He believes that the form of crisis intervention should be consistent with the already defined functions of one's chosen profession.

[3] Caplan, *Principles of Preventive Psychiatry,* p. 48.

He does not recommend a direct transfer from the methods of perception, assessment, and psychotherapy from the psychiatrist or psychologist to the minister. The basic professional role of the clergyman should always be maintained in order for him to be of greatest value to the person who understands himself as talking with a minister. A direct transfer of techniques might entail the modification of perspective integral to the role and functioning of the minister to such a degree that he is robbed of his own unique and helpful perceptions and approaches.[4] This does not mean, of course, that we have nothing to learn from the psychiatric professional. But we must work out with some clarity what we may adopt with value for our understanding and technique without damage to our fundamental role. Certainly, too, there should be beneath every professional role a genuinely human basis for the sensitive perception of the situation and for methods of dealing with the person and his problem.

On the other side of the coin, it should be appropriately noted that the way in which ministers have traditionally functioned and related to persons in need could be studied by other mental health professionals to their advantage. An interesting article by McGee has outlined four considerations that he feels are an absolute necessity for mental health workers in order to utilize in the most effective way certain techniques of crisis intervention. Although he himself makes no reference to it at all, he makes a superb case for the minister as the present number one crisis counseling professional, and uses the model of the minister's typical functioning in order to make his point in regard to the

[4] *Ibid.*, p. 52.

transformation of the operation of at least much of the present community mental health program.

The first consideration that he mentions is *location.* The mental health worker "must be located in and involved with a specific community or communities." [5] A person in crisis is much more likely to seek help and to do so more rapidly when this is the case. In any community, few facilities are more universally present or more easily recognized than the church building and few professionals more visible than the clergy, who have a double tie with the community of faith itself through persons' voluntary association with the church and with the larger community through the minister's active participation in it. Every minister has had the experience of having people come to him for help simply because they live down the block from the church or were just driving by and saw it or had seen or heard or met him at some community gathering.

The second consideration is *availability.* A person in distress "must be guaranteed an effective contact . . . rapidly and *during the period of crisis*, not two or three weeks hence." [6] McGee turns thumbs down on the Monday through Friday, nine to five operation as an appropriate schedule for meeting crises. People simply do not pay attention to typical clinic hours as a format for the production of their own crises. The minister, as all of us know, has never been accused, certainly not by his own family, of keeping such hours rigidly. He is available. The importance of immediate access to a helping person at the time of crisis is emphasized by several professionals in the field, pointing to the value of the

---

[5] Thomas F. McGee, "Some Basic Considerations in Crisis Intervention," *Community Mental Health Journal*, IV (1968), 323.
   [6] *Ibid.*

rapid reduction of some of the dangers of crisis, and the value to the rapid establishing of a firm therapeutic working relationship.[7]

The third necessary factor for the fuller meeting of people's crisis needs is *mobility*. "The mental health professional who merely waits in a mental health facility for an individual in crisis to appear is not prepared to engage in comprehensive crisis intervention." [8] Again, the conscientious and dedicated minister is a model: visiting in the homes, getting to know persons, opening doors for counseling, sensing needs at an early stage, visiting in the hospital where most persons are experiencing mild to severe crisis,[9] being on call to go to an unbelievable variety of places when asked to do so, taking the initiative to intervene by going to persons wherever they are and whenever he has reason to believe that there is need.

The fourth consideration is *flexibility* of procedure. By this McGee is referring to the effective use of the telephone specifically and the ready acceptance of "walk-ins" just as quickly as possible. Interestingly, he feels it necessary to point out that these and other procedures are not demeaning and beneath one's professional status.[10] This latter thought had probably never

[7] Neble Nikolaus, "Essential Elements in Short-term Treatment," *Social Casework*, LII (June, 1971), 380; Kalis *et al*. "Precipitating Stress as a Focus," p. 225; David M. Kaplan, "Observations on Crisis Theory and Practice," *Social Casework* XLIX (March, 1968), 155.

[8] McGee, "Some Basic Considerations," 323.

[9] Donna G. Aguilera, "Crisis: Moment of Truth," *Journal of Psychiatric Nursing and Mental Health Services*, IX (May, 1971), 23-25; Irene M. Burnside, "Crisis Intervention with Geriatric Hospitalized Patients," *Journal of Psychiatric Nursing and Mental Health Services*, VIII (March, 1970), 17-20.

[10] McGee, "Some Basic Considerations," p. 324.

occurred to most ministers, whose usual training and inclination have combined to lead them to do whatever they could whenever they could if it seemed to be the best thing to do for the person in need. Certainly counseling and follow-up on the telephone and accepting people for immediate counseling when they walk into the church is standard operating procedure.

Most ministers will not only accept McGee's points, they will recognize their own methods of operating which could very well have served as the source of his suggestions. Most ministers function in these ways because they are persons who genuinely desire to help others, who have received out of their own tradition forms of serving that have proved themselves to be useful, and who keep an openness to new forms and a readiness to experiment with them and adopt them when they prove to be useful. Of course, what has been discussed here has related primarily to the minister's role and context and, to some extent, motivation. Still crucial are those elements of his functioning that grow out of the underlying human factors of the minister as helper, his own level of adjustment, his manner of relating to other persons, his warmth, genuineness, courage, openness. The whole issue of the helper as a human being and how he or she contributes to or takes away from the growth of the person seeking help must be examined honestly.

Many ministers who graduated from seminary some years ago can remember their first courses in pastoral care and counseling. Among the first important things that we learned was that pastoral counseling was not (1) immediately and automatically applying the forms, symbols, rites, and sacraments of the church as the answer to all problems, nor was it (2) immediate advice as to the course of action a person should take. Once beyond that, a major impression from what we learned was that if we applied the methodology of nondirective counseling, a number of people would be helped significantly, the great majority would be helped some, and no one would be injured. With qualifications, that may have been very close to the truth. But what happened with most of us when we were let loose on real people with real problems was that we had no supervision, no guidelines to determine whether we were applying that methodology consistently, no data relating the methodology to the *person* who was using it. As a result we fell into many errors, yet continued to believe that at the very worst there would be a few people whom we would not be able to help. Further research over the years has shown us how wrong we were, that as a matter of fact, counseling is like marriage, it is for better or for worse. In fact, it is like any relationship. It never stays the same; it is always in process. Persons in distress likewise do not remain precisely where they are. They get better or they get worse, and the helping persons have much to do with the direction they go.[11] Research evidence smashes the idea that just any sort of person may learn certain ideas and techniques and thereby become an effective counselor of others. The hypothesis that has been tested, and so far upheld, is that "all effective interpersonal processes share a common core of conditions conducive to facilitative human experiences."[12] These conditions are not just something that we do, but are reflections of who we are. It is a rather obvious fact that the counselor is a key ingredient in the process in that he offers a model of a

[11] Carkhuff, *Helping and Human Relations*, Vol. II, pp. 5, 7-8.
[12] *Ibid.*, Vol. II, p. 7.

person who is living effectively. There are crucial elements of the relationship necessary for the growth of persons in distress that the counselor cannot simply produce by something he *does*, unless somehow that is what he *is*, unless his behavior in the relationship is an authentic expression of his own being.[13]

Carkhuff refers to the three R's of helping which are appropriate to discuss in the context of the minister's intervention in crisis:

1. The *right* of the helper to intervene in the life of another
2. The *responsibility* of the helper once he has intervened
3. The *role* the helper must assume in helping another individual, and at the same time, the various role conflicts he encounters in attempting to implement the responsibilities implied by intervention [14]

We ministers have not too often questioned our *right* to enter into the lives of other persons in a variety of ways, both by invitation and at our own initiative. Somehow we have assumed this right as a proper and inherent given in our being ministers. Carkhuff, however, basing his conclusions on a growing body of research data, states that this right must be based on our ability to help, not just our traditional role. This means that we must be functioning at higher levels of effectiveness ourselves in the relevant areas of concern. "Only the person who is alive and growing can enable the struggling person to choose life at the life and death crisis points." [15] The clergyman should not be in the ministry or in his counseling work primarily to fulfill, in these rather temporary pastoral care and counseling

[13] *Ibid.*, Vol. I, p. 45.
[14] *Ibid.*, Vol. I, pp. xi-xiv.
[15] *Ibid.*, Vol. I, p. xii.

relationships, those needs of his own that are quite unfulfilled in the large areas of his personal life or to find intimacy that he knows in no other place. Otherwise, he may end up helping neither himself nor others.

The matter of *responsibility* follows hard on the heels of this statement. The person who intervenes primarily out of his own lack of fulfillment acts in a distorted manner that is a reflection of his incompleteness, and thus his procedures in relating to others will be more designed to serve him than to serve other persons. He will subtract from the responses of the person in need far more than he will add, thereby increasing the other person's distortions rather than reducing them. This speaks of responsibility, initially to ourselves, in regard to our own growth, health, meaningful relationships, *in order that* we may have something mainly ourselves, to offer to the other.

The matter of *role* is a particularly important issue for us ministers, for we have a long history, a tradition, that tells us and the larger society something about who the clergyman is. Without going into detail here, we need to clarify the difference between what certain of our functions as clergymen are and who we really are as individual human beings. We need to be able to utilize the symbolic power of our role, but without hiding behind it or exploiting people with it. Our *role responsibility* as pastoral counselors is a commitment to do all we can that will translate into benefits for the person who needs help. Our movement in the process is always from the role at first to the person later, a personal relationship "in which neither person allows himself or the other to be less than he can be." [16]

[16] *Ibid.*, Vol. I, p. xiv.

All this leads to an obvious conclusion. The minister cannot be an effectual crisis counselor merely by learning theory and techniques from a book. He must grow as a person. One of the central functions of the minister at all times, and most certainly in his counseling, is to provide for others a model of one who has a purpose in life, who has satisfying relationships, who is able to utilize his insights in appropriate action. Most of us as ministers have very little choice as to whether we will or will not be involved with persons in crisis. The only choice is how well we are going to function for the other's benefit. The obligation is laid upon us to grow in the direction of being that kind of person who contributes more to the helping process than we take away from it, by taking advantage of whatever opportunities are available to us: clinical training, supervision of our counseling by another professional, growth groups, individual or group therapy.

Carkhuff summarizes it succinctly: "Perhaps the point on which to conclude a consideration of the counselor's contribution to helping processes is the point at which all effective helping begins, that is, with an integrated and growing person, one who is personally productive and creative, one whose life is dominated by personal meaning and fulfillment. Without such persons in the helping role there is no hope in the world or for the world." [17]

THE BASIC CONDITIONS
FOR EFFECTIVE COUNSELING

The obvious implication of what has been discussed about the person of the counselor himself is that no

[17] *Ibid.*, Vol. I, p. 45.

person in need can reach a higher level of functioning than that which the helping person has achieved. Therefore, that which the minister has to give in counseling is primarily himself. This is not to say that techniques, the knowledge of what kinds of statements to respond to at what times and in what verbal forms and what sorts of nonverbal interventions to make, are unimportant, but these are always conveyed through the vehicle of a person in relationship with another person.

There is a growing body of evidence, growing out of research begun by Rogers, continued by Truax and Carkhuff, and elaborated in more detail with even newer data by Carkhuff,[18] which indicates that regardless of theoretical orientation or style or technique, there are certain critical ingredients of the successful psychotherapeutic relationship. When these ingredients are present, persons in need are helped, and when these ingredients are not part of the relationship and process to an adequate degree, there are negative results.[19]

These essential ingredients, referred to as the "facilitative conditions," are what the counselor introduces into the helping relationship.[20] These are just as relevant in the relationship and process of crisis intervention as they are in longer-term counseling.

The first, most important, and foundational condition that must be provided by the counselor is *accurate empathy* and its accurate communication. This is central from beginning to end, and without it there can hardly *be* any other conditions. And to the extent that

[18] *On Becoming a Person*, pp. 60-64. Charles Truax and Robert R. Carkhuff, *Toward Effective Counseling and Psychotherapy* (Chicago: Aldine Publishing Company, 1967), pp. 31-43; Carkhuff, *Helping and Human Relations*, Vol. I, pp. 33-45.

[19] *Helping and Human Relations*, Vol. I, p. 42.

[20] *Ibid.*, Vol. I, pp. 35-39, 173-95; Vol. II, 82-95.

there are some of the others, without empathy they are useless. The counselor must be able to perceive, sense, feel what the other person is feeling, and must communicate in verbal and nonverbal ways that he is where the other person is emotionally. This does not mean, obviously, that we have the same quantity of rage, depression, lust, fear, and other emotions of the distressed person at that moment, but we communicate that we are aware of what his feelings are, the intensity of them, and that we are somehow sharing this experience with him.

A response by the counselor that is minimally facilitative is one that is interchangeable both in content and affect with the statement of the person in need. The response becomes more facilitative to the extent that the counselor perceives and communicates how the person really feels beneath the surface, or how the person feels in addition to the emotion verbally expressed, thereby enabling the person to experience and express his feelings in a manner he was previously unable to do.

The second essential ingredient of all helping relationships is *respect,* the extent to which the helper genuinely cares about the other, is committed to his worth as a person, is convinced of his potential for growth, and communicates this by commitment to the counseling process and in other ways in and through the relationship.

The third facilitative condition is *concreteness.* This has to do with the amount of help the counselor gives to the other in terms of enabling him to be very specific, concrete, about his feelings, experiences, language, meanings, not allowing him to "speak in general," or "feel in general." The counselor assists this concreteness by a variety of means, ranging from direct questions or instructions or suggestions to reflections. For example, a person might say something like, "I've been feeling pretty bad a lot recently." The counselor's response might be: "I can sense from the way you say this that you've been hurting and are even hurting right now. This must be very discouraging to you. I wonder if you could give me an example of this and just exactly what bad feelings you are talking about." Rather sophisticated counselees might use popular psychological jargon: "I seem to be projecting a lot today." The counselor is obligated to respond: "I wonder if you could tell me what you mean by projecting and give me an example of how you have been doing it."

The fourth and fifth facilitative conditions are closely linked with one another: *genuineness* and *self-disclosure*. Genuineness is both the means and the end of counseling. To the extent that there is a correspondence between the experience, the awareness of the experience, and the communication of that awareness in the helping person, there is a tendency for the same awareness and communication to develop in the person being helped. The person who is genuine is freely and deeply himself in responding to experiences of all types and has an ability to utilize negative feelings for the helpful exploration of the relationship. A lack of genuineness is characterized either by being out of touch with one's own feelings or being incapable or unwilling to express them in helpful forms to another, or actually communicating in some way negative feelings which, however authentic, are so strong as to be harmful to the other person. A high level of defensiveness is also characteristic of a low level of genuineness. Interfering with the expression of genuineness are an exaggerated professionalism, a rehearsed quality to one's responses, or responses according to a prescribed role rather than expressing what one personally feels or means. Self-disclosure is, of course, a function of genuineness. It refers to the degree to which the counselor allows himself to be known as a human being, being open to revealing himself personally either in response to questions of the person seeking help or even, when the relationship has been well established, taking the initiative in an appropriate context to disclose important areas of his own life and selfhood in a way constructive to the counselee.

The sixth essential ingredient is *confrontation*. It should be made clear that this does not refer to verbal shock treatment, the hard-hitting interpretation, frequently a guess, about what is taking place in the person's life. Genuine confrontation is based on the assumption that a person needs and, down underneath all defenses, wants an undistorted external observation and evaluation of his behavior. Confrontation is simply the pointing out in a clear manner, through indirect and direct questioning as well as by reflective statement, any of three forms of discrepancy in the counselee: those between his insights and actions, between his own self-concept and his ideal concept, and between his experience of himself and the counselor's experience of him.

The final facilitative condition in the helping process is termed *immediacy*, referring to the way both the helper and the person in need are experiencing the relationship between them in the present moment. The counselor recognizes the possibility that expressions by the counselee, which are apparently about events or relationships outside of the counseling session, might in fact be referring to the relationship right then and there. This recognition is verbalized in an explicit manner, the connection is made between what the counselee has said and how it may have meaning for this present relationship, and the two persons enter into an exploration of what is taking place between them. There are two benefits of immediacy. First, it provides an intensity of experience between two persons that is seldom a part of people's lives. Second, it provides a model to the counselee of a person who understands and acts on his experience, both of his own impact on another and the other's impact on him.

Time and further research may show that there are additional factors at work in personal relationships that are essential to the growth of the individuals involved, but at the present time the evidence supports the conclusion that the presence of these seven in at least a minimally facilitative degree are necessary for the helping process. It is upon this foundation that the crisis methodology specifically must be built if it is to produce the necessary interruption of the downward spiral of crisis and lead to positive growth.

THE PROCESS AND METHODS OF CRISIS COUNSELING

Having considered the goal of crisis counseling, the role and the person of the minister, and the essential ingredients of the helping process which are a function both of the minister's personhood and training, what are the specific methods of crisis intervention that seem to be appropriate for the minister to consider as having the possibility of integration into his psychotherapeutic role? Jacobson, the director of the Benjamin Rush Center in Los Angeles, makes clear the context of the therapeutic approach: "The advantages to be gained from crisis therapy can be maximized when the patient's crisis becomes the deliberate focus of the treatment." [21] This approach is in contrast with many traditional psychotherapeutic methods that either allow the person in need to choose his own point of departure and route in the elaboration of his condition and situation or that move into an investigation of long-standing personality patterns, including pathology. The relevance for the minister of the focus on the contemporary issue rather than on deep-seated psychopathology rooted in early childhood seems obvious when one considers the role of the minister, his training and the time he has available. To say this, though, is not to indicate that he has no need for thorough training in this approach or that he must be content with helping people in only a superficial way.

Rapoport points out that the three areas of need in crisis define the tasks of intervention. First, the distorted perceptions of the person in crisis make it necessary that the problem which leads to the call for help be clarified. As a result of identifying the external and internal events that have led to the disruption, cognitive restructuring should take place and should lead toward a more rational response to the situation. Second, since strong emotions are also being experienced, these need to be discharged in appropriate ways. This task is facilitated by the acceptance of the feelings by the counselor at the same time he is helping the person understand the source of these reactions. Finally, since there is some amount of therapeutic force built into the

[21] Gerald Jacobson, "Crisis Theory and Treatment Strategy: Some Sociocultural and Psychodynamic Considerations," *The Journal of Nervous and Mental Diseases*, CXLI (August, 1965), 215.

ordinary networks of human relationships, social structures and institutions, and routines and rituals, the person in crisis should be helped to identify and utilize those that are most appropriate for himself and his circumstances.[22]

There are a number of conceptual schemes that can contain the total crisis intervention process with goals such as these. One of the simple and useful frameworks is that provided by Warren Jones, a psychiatrist who has had much experience and great success in training lay persons to do crisis counseling. He refers to the A-B-C method:

A—Achieve contact with the client.
B—Boil down the problem to its essentials.
C—Cope actively through an inventory of the client's ingenuity and resources.[23]

Taking his key words and filling in the details, the total process might look like the following:

Contact	*Focus*	*Cope*
1. Establish the relationship.	5. Explore the present situation.	7. Inventory problem-solving resources.
2. Identify the presenting problem and the precipitating event.	6. Identify the threat.	8. Assist in decision-making.
3. Assist catharsis.		9. Emphasize relationships with others.
4. Build hopeful expectation.		10. Summarize new learning.

[22] Rapoport, "The State of Crisis," pp. 29-30.
[23] Warren A. Jones, "The A-B-C Method of Crisis Management," *Mental Hygiene*, LII (January, 1968), 87.

It will naturally be understood that while the above outline does in general give an accurate picture of the chronological process, the individual steps themselves are not always that sharply delineated from one another, nor do they always move smoothly and in an unbroken progression. Several steps may be in process at one given time, or movement backward to a prior stage may often take place. This should become clear as the details of the procedure emerge.

Contact

The first issue of significance is the *establishment* of *a relationship of trust*. All counseling has already been clearly enough defined in relational terms, and it is no less important in crisis counseling than in any other type. Yet it is obvious that although this is mentioned first, it is not a step separate from several of the rest. How is relationship established in the first place? By the counselor's actively showing interest and concern. And how is this done? By encouraging the person to tell his or her story, by responsive listening, the communication of accurate empathy, the expression of warmth, the eliciting of emotional expression. As these lead to a rapid diminishing of anxiety, the person in crisis is rewarded by what is taking place and the value of the relationship is reinforced.[24] In other words, the therapeutic relationship desired is established by accomplishing the other three steps of the process listed under "Contact": identifying the presenting problem and the precipitating event, expediting catharsis, and building a hopeful expectation. This relationship then

[24] Thomas N. Rusk, "Opportunity and Technique in Crisis Psychiatry," *Comprehensive Psychiatry*, XII (May, 1971), 252.

becomes the leverage that the minister can utilize in assisting and supporting the person as he or she begins to move into the difficult task of behavioral change and the sense of risk which it entails.[25]

An absolutely essential task of the early stage of crisis intervention is to *identify the presenting problem and the precipitating event.* What is the immediate problem? What is the source of the present distress? Relevant questions to stimulate this process are: Why are you here? Why did you come at this time? What do you want or expect me to do for you? What has been happening in your life within the past two weeks? When did you begin to feel this way, or when did you begin to feel worse? What is new in your life situation? What persons have been involved? This procedure is a part of the determination of *whether* there is a crisis at all, as well as a necessary early step if it is discovered that in fact there *is.* The questions listed here and others like them are an attempt to determine whether the person's present feeling of distress, despair, depression, tension, anxiety, panic, whatever term or combination of terms may be used to describe the feelings that the person is now experiencing, are of recent origin or whether they are rather persistent, long-standing, or regularly recurring patterns in the individual's life, and if of recent origin, whether they can be linked with a specific precipitating event that has occurred only a short time before.

If the feelings are discovered to be a persistent or recurring part of the person's life over a long period of time, or if no precipitating event can be found, it is assumed that there is no present crisis. The task is

[25] *Ibid.*

81

then to determine what type of help the person does need at this time: long-term counseling, occasional supportive counseling, referral to another professional or agency. Then that procedure should be pursued.

However, if the distress is of recent origin, if it came on rather suddenly, and if a precipitating event can be identified, then one should continue with the specified methodology of crisis intervention. It should be emphasized that even though persons in crisis are aware that something is wrong at the moment, they may or may not be able without considerable assistance to discover what set off this emotional response and the sense of inability to cope. It is the crisis counselor's responsibility to help the person pin down as precisely as possible the precipitating stress. It is usually necessary to lead the person in distress into some recognition of the defenses that he is utilizing as he endeavors to cover up the nature of the crisis and the emotions surrounding it. It must constantly be kept in mind that the focus is not on what has led to the preconditioning of the personality which has responded to the distress with maladaptive behavior, *but on what the present stress itself is*. Frequently the source of it is to be found in a disintegrating relationship or one that is losing its power to satisfy the needs of the person. Therefore, specific questions concerning significant relationships are in order. In many instances unresolved grief or other forms of separation are discovered as a major dynamic force, although it should always be recognized that the situations or events to which persons can respond with a rapidly rising gradient of anxiety or the rapid onset of depression are many.

An illustration of the onset of crisis, its identification as such, and the location of the precipitating event is afforded by a woman who walked into the office of a church situated in the downtown section of a city. This is a common enough occurrence for any pastor, and particularly those in the heart of a city. She showed obvious signs of distress, nervousness, considerable confusion.

The minister made some verbal recognition of his perception of her distress and asked how it was she happened to come into his office. She replied that she had been walking along the street window-shopping when quite suddenly it seemed as if everything were beginning to take on a sense of unreality. She could see the people, but they seemed to be unreal. Increasingly she felt as if her whole world were going to pieces. She looked around her desperately, searching for something that would save her. She saw the church, walked into the chapel, and after a moment saw the sign saying that a minister was available, so she came in for help, and she needed it now.

The assessment by the minister was that the very first help that she needed was assistance in expressing her present feelings of panic and her sense of unreality as fully and concretely as possible in relationship with a person who could in some sense share with her the terror that she felt but who himself was not actually in terror that the world was in fact crumbling, who could receive and participate in her strong emotion but who was not threatened by it, who showed confidence that the world was real, and who could concretize this in the reality of their present relationship. So there was the encouragement by the minister to her to express her emotions, to tell her story about today, as he sought to communicate accurate empathy, continually emphasize concreteness, and take the occasion to refer to the reality of his care for her in the context of the present process.

So the questions of why she came and why she came today were clearly answered. Relationship was established as she expressed her feelings and much catharsis was accomplished. After only ten or fifteen minutes she was feeling better and was clearly "coming back into the world again." This perception of her was stated by the minister, and she confirmed it. The search for the precipitating event was then consciously begun, because it had not come out in what she had said up to this point. First, the minister asked if she could think of anything that might have made her feel this way. She could think of nothing. Then he asked, "Can you think of anything at all that has happened in the last week or two which was quite upsetting to you at the time?" Her mouth literally fell open, and she exclaimed, "How did you know?" Of course, he did not know. He was simply following procedure. The conversation then went something like the following:

Minister: Could you tell me about it?

Woman: No, I really couldn't. I don't want to talk about it. (*Silence*)

Minister: Perhaps this is what you need to talk about.

Woman: Oh, I can't. It's just too painful. (*Silence*)

Minister: It's becoming clear to me that this is probably the pain that has caused this reaction of yours today since it's so intense you feel that you can't discuss it.

Woman: I just *can't* talk about it. (*Silence*)

Minister: It seems to me that you're going to have to make the choice either to experience the pain of talking with me about it here today, and get it out and over with and really

84

taken care of, or else you'll have to experience the panic and sense of unreality you
felt earlier today, and perhaps experience it
over and over again, and be uncertain about
the outcome. (*Silence*)

Woman: All right. I'll try to do it. I don't know
whether I can or not. It'll hurt so much.

Minister: I know it will. I'll try to help you.

It can be observed that although the minister was
sensitive to her pain and sought to be tender, he persistently pushed her in the direction of expressing the
experience aloud in spite of the hurt. He would have
been unfair to her to allow her pain to become a reason
for not talking about it.

So then she began to talk about a most meaningful
and helpful relationship that she had established with
the counselor she had been seeing regularly for over a
period of some two years. This led to some recounting
of her own background, which was one of emotional
problems all her life, a tenuous hold on reality, no
friends, lonely, never married, minimally effectual in a
job, a long history of therapy. But here in the relationship with this counselor she felt that she had found
someone who had been supportive to her, whom she
could count on, whom she had become quite dependent upon. In their last session, however, some ten
days before, she discovered with horror that his wife had
recently divorced him. She was crushed. He had been
her ideal, her support, but now this terrible thing had
taken place. She stated that she could never go back
to him again. She had lost him. In this discussion, with
its additional outpouring of pain, she also saw how
her discovery of this fact had initiated the feelings that

85

had led to her present experience. The precipitating event had been identified.

This initial phase of a crisis intervention session also illustrates quite clearly how *emotional catharsis* takes place as a natural part of the process itself. It is always important for the counselor to facilitate the recognition and expression of strong negative emotions such as hostility, hate, anxiety, guilt, grief, and others that have distorted a person's perception of himself and his situation to such a degree that he cannot make effective decisions and perform stress-reducing actions. Catharsis can be expedited by a stated perception of the person's affective responses: "You seem to be quite sad." "You appear to be ready to cry." Or questions like: "What are you feeling as you talk about this?" The purpose goes beyond the mere expression of emotions, although that in itself is necessary, and should lead to the clear and specific identification of them and the person or situation toward whom they are directed. Where negative feelings are directed toward the counselor or negative attitudes form a barrier, these must be recognized and talked about and settled before other steps are taken. As quickly as possible, though, the focus must move from emotional catharsis to an understanding of the concrete factors involved in this particular crisis and the making of the decisions necessary to deal with one's present situation. The therapist is not to offer primarily an opportunity merely to reduce tension or to be a target for vague emotions or distorted attitudes, although this is frequently an early part of the relationship. The job at hand is to help the person deal effectively with his problem.

A fourth major task of the "Contact" stage of the crisis intervention process is to *build a sense of hope-*

ful expectation. There are a variety of ways in which this may be done, including the attitude of the counselor, occasionally his specific words, as well as the crisis intervention procedure itself. Contrary to some approaches to counseling, the person in crisis is not allowed to talk about anything at all and to take his own time in doing it. Without making the situation tense, it is made clear that there is no time to waste. At the walk-in clinic of the Benjamin Rush Center in Los Angeles, persons who come for aid are led to an understanding from the very beginning that they are to have no more than six sessions, and that something is really expected to happen in this time. Morley summarizes it, "On entry, plan discharge." [26] This number of sessions, if spaced weekly, is consistent with the usual time pattern of the crisis, placing the type of limitation that tends to push the participants away from wasting time, reduce dependency, and create positive expectation in the mind of the distressed person. The possibility of change, and therefore hope, is affirmed. Unfortunately, pastors are often the inheritors of what has been programmed into many psychotherapists during their training. This is the assumption that results obtained from long-term therapy are inevitably better and longer lasting than those growing out of brief therapy.[27] To the contrary, the results of crisis intervention are clear evidence for the genuine and lasting aid given to persons by this method. Morley states his conviction "that this approach is not a 'second best' technique, but probably the most effective technique which can be utilized with crisis." [28]

[26] "Treatment of the Patient in Crisis."
[27] C. Knight Aldrich, "Brief Psychotherapy: A Reappraisal of Some Theoretical Assumptions," *American Journal of Psychiatry*, CXXV (1968), 585.
[28] "Treatment of the Patient in Crisis."

Aldrich believes that the attitude communicated either nonverbally or verbally by the counselor to the person in regard to his condition and situation may be a self-fulfilling prophecy. "When 'long-term' treatment is recommended to a patient, he is in effect told that he is not expected to be able in a short time to develop the capacity to cope with his residual problems." [29] The crisis counselor should be alert to pick up cues in the very first interview that a person is able and willing to cope with his problems. Then the counselor must work with the person in need to capitalize on these positive aspects of himself. While avoiding a false optimism and a superficial reassurance, the person's present activity in seeking help should be affirmed clearly to him, his present strengths pointed out and reinforced, and the expectation of change within a short period of time communicated. Rusk states: "Hope, like confidence, is contagious." [30] It is also an essential ingredient of the crisis counseling process, because this expectation of positive results becomes one of the prime motivators for therapeutic change.[31]

Focus

The second major stage of the process is that of focusing on the present situation, the source of the stress, and the attempt to identify the nature of the threat to the individual. Actually these are not two distinct and separable steps, *exploration* and *identification of threat*. They are separated in this way simply to emphasize what must be accomplished. As a result of their

[29] "Brief Psychotherapy," p. 590.
[30] "Opportunity and Technique," p. 253.
[31] *Ibid.*

intensive study of the precipitating stress of their forty patients and the subsequent therapy, Kalis concluded "that a focus on the factors precipitating the *request for help* can be therapeutic" in enabling most persons to come through the period of disruption and maladaptive behavior successfully.[32] She goes on to outline the procedure as the clear identification and isolation of the factors as has just been done here under "identifying the presenting problem and the precipitating event," then moving on to a more thorough formulation of the total problem and a working through of the unique personal meaning of the precipitating stress.[33] It is this procedure which will now be elaborated.

Basic to the entire process is the development of what Rusk calls "consensual formulation," the person in crisis and the counselor working together toward a conceptualizing of the immediate past and the present events to create an understanding of the crisis to which they both agree.[34] If the distressed person has difficulty in grasping some of the interaction between events, relationships, and his feelings, the counselor may need to state the core of the problem as he sees it in as direct and clear a way as possible. Of course, he encourages feedback from the person as to whether this makes sense to him and invites correction from the other. The purpose is, of course, to make the dilemma conscious and put it into words. Only when this has been done can the distressed person become capable of moving into the later stages of the process and examine various alternative methods of dealing with the present crisis, of making decisions concerning those alternatives which

[32] "Precipitating Stress as a Focus," p. 225.
[33] *Ibid.*
[34] "Opportunity and Technique," p. 258.

seem most appropriate, and of mobilizing what ego resources are available to him.

One of the major methods that the crisis counselor
uses in this phase of detailed exploration of the present
situation is referred to as focusing, the filtering out by
the counselor of extraneous material and keeping the
session close to the particular problem at hand. Delv-
ing into one's distant past is discouraged, as the counselor moves the conversation back to the present: contemporary emotions, relationships, frustrations, conflicts,
losses. Clues concerning the crisis are picked up from
what the person says, how he says it, facial expression,
gestures; and focusing comments are made to the person on the basis of these clues. In this way, the counselor
aids the person to be honest with himself, to select the
most relevant material to deal with, and to become an
observer of himself.

The process of focusing may be visualized by the
following diagram:

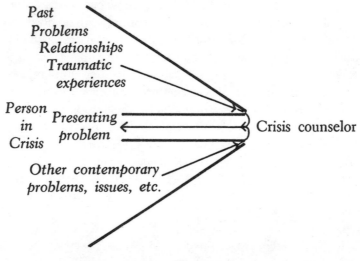

A person in crisis naturally brings with him his whole past, including whatever unsolved problems might be there, as well as contemporary problems and ineffective behavior patterns which might not be related to the present crisis. The responsibility of the crisis counselor, when any issue from the past is raised, or any contemporary material that is not readily identified as being a factor in the crisis is introduced, is to seek to relate this material to the presenting problem and its precipitating event in some way. Focusing statements and questions may sound like: "Your bringing up this memory of what happened to you in high school makes me wonder if you see it relating to your present problem." Or, "I wonder if you sense some relationship between what you are describing about your problems at work and this particular situation with your wife that you came to see me about."

The counselor picks up on any material from whatever direction it may come and channels it back to the person in distress in terms of the clearly identified crisis problem. If together the two of them determine that it is not related, it is dropped. It may be an issue worthy of further investigation later; it may be a problem that needs to be solved, and further counseling may be indicated. But if it is not a part of the *presenting problem* at hand, time is not taken to discuss it now. The *crisis*, and it alone, is the focus. If some issue from the past is seen to be connected with the crisis in some way, then it is to be explored, not because it is past, but because it is an element of the present situation. The major purpose of this stage and the technique of focusing is to explore every aspect of the crisis—the total situation, contemporary relationships—in order to make it just as clear as possible to the person precisely what is taking place. An important goal of this exploration is to identify the threat, why it is that the precipitating event stimulated this particular reaction. Rusk points to an important emphasis when he suggests as one of the areas of intensive exploration that of unsatisfied needs. What changes in the contemporary life situation have resulted in formerly met needs being met no longer? Especially, what person or persons may be disappointing this individual? [35]

The woman who came into the church office seeking immediate help had now portrayed herself not only as an individual in present crisis but also as one who had a life history of problems. It became important then to separate out the long-term personal and social maladaptive behavior from that which was crisis related only. Focusing was a major technique in making this necessary distinction. Then the question was raised, "Why is it that finding out about your counselor's divorce caused you to feel that things were unreal, that the world was dissolving or going to pieces?"

A summary of the discussion and its conclusion led through an analysis of her needs as a person, how these needs were in some way being met in the therapeutic relationship, what it was she had imagined her counselor to be, based on what she needed to believe that he was, and how the reality of who he was conflicted with her construction of what reality should be for her.

She was a person who had learned that she needed to be dependent on others. Her fantasy was that only a strong, well-adjusted (read "perfect") person would be capable of sustaining her life as a person, and that her counselor was such an individual. But now she had discovered that he could not even take care of his own

[35] *Ibid.*, p. 257.

life; he was the sort of person whose wife could not live with him. Divorce was wrong. If she were dependent for the maintenance of her selfhood, her world, upon one whom she now perceived as a man who was not omnicompetent and all "good," what was left of her world? It was unreal; it was crumbling beneath her. Essentially, of course, it was the experience of her selfhood being unsupported and coming apart and the natural perception of threat under these circumstances. As this was discussed, she increasingly understood and could articulate what was happening to her. Her present situation was thoroughly explored, and she was able to identify why it was she had felt the way she did, why the event posed the threat which she had felt. In addition, the phase of detailed exploration included a discussion about her unrealistic concept that only a perfect person could help her and her fantasy of her counselor as having been perfect. This naturally extended into further conversation about what it is that any person needs to help another and a realistic appraisal of both the role and the genuine humanity, including both the strengths and weaknesses, of any professional person.

Cope

The final stage of the crisis intervention process is coping. Decision and action, doing something about one's situation, is the goal of the whole procedure.

The first phase involves making an *inventory of problem-solving resources,* seeking those strengths within the person himself that he has lost sight of in the midst of the distortions of the crisis and those resources outside one's self, one's usual pattern of social relationships, the persons close to him (family, friends, coworkers), community helpers (ministers, doctors, lawyers), or agencies designed to help with specific problems (vocational counseling and employment, emergency loan, housing, Alcoholics Anonymous or Al Anon, drug treatment).

One way into such an inventory—and actually one that has been taking shape chronologically well before this stage in the total intervention process—is to listen very carefully for references to occasions in the person's past that are similar to this present one in any way. If none has been mentioned, the counselor at this point might ask directly, "Does this remind you of the way you have ever felt before?" This is the first time that the counselor has taken the initiative to explore the past. He does so now with a specific twofold purpose in mind. First, if the person has felt like this before, it is of some value for him to add to his perspective on the present crisis the fact that he has been in crisis before, lived through it, and come out of it. This reinforces an attitude of hope toward the successful outcome of the present situation and an awareness of inner strength which has probably been lost sight of. Second, a discussion of how the person was enabled to resolve the earlier crisis might suggest some methods of dealing with the contemporary one. If methods that were effective earlier have already been tried this time without success, an analysis should be made of why this is the case. The person should be pushed to look for inner strengths and to suggest resources outside himself. His initial rejection of certain persons or agencies out of hand should not be allowed. His objections must be dealt with on a rational basis, and serious reconsideration of all available resources should be made.

The latter part of the inventory begins to overlap with the next steps, the *decision to utilize* certain of these resources and not some of the others. At this time, the person in crisis should be encouraged to think of every possible decision he can make and action he can perform in order to change his situation and condition in some way. At times this is relatively simple, at other times extremely difficult. There are many options open to some people in most situations. With other people a great deal of imagination and effort must be put forth in order to find the caring persons in their lives, an appropriate agency that can do something constructive with this person with this problem. The first effort should be to get the distressed person to do his own planning, without inhibition or selectivity at this point. After he has exhausted the listing of alternatives, only then will the counselor suggest any that have occurred to him. While this procedure is obviously not non-directive, neither is it advice-giving. It is not hearing the person out and then telling him what action to take, except in unusual circumstances, one of which will be illustrated later. Here, as throughout the whole crisis counseling process, the person must be made aware again and again that his problem and the solution to it are his responsibility. The counselor is merely a process stimulator. Rusk's classic statement should be memorized: "The golden rule for the therapist in crisis intervention is to do for others that which they cannot do for themselves and no more!" [36] Therefore, when the person in distress has been encouraged and even pushed to present all possible options for ways of dealing with his current situation, only then are other alternatives introduced by the counselor. These are laid

[36] *Ibid.*, p. 251.

alongside those already made by the person in distress. "You have mentioned this and this, but I wonder if you have thought of so and so."

Then all these alternatives are discussed with a view to evaluating what is significantly related to the crisis and its possible resolution. What is possible? What is feasible? What would be the probable results? "What could you do? How would you feel while you were doing this? What do you suppose would happen if you did that? What would be the best option to try first?" After these issues are thoroughly explored, the person must make some decision to do something, with the counselor taking a firm stand against a do-nothing inertia. The decision should be the counselee's own. He must make it, then commit himself to following it through. The counselor intrudes to counteract a decision only if he clearly sees that it could result in significant harm to the counselee or someone else (murder, drug use of certain kinds, robbery, suicide), or if he feels that the possibilities of harm in other ways are so great (running away, divorce) that the action might at least be considered premature at this time and should therefore be postponed until some further movement is made by acting upon other decisions first. Otherwise, after possible results are fully discussed, the decision is made, the action initiated. Even if in some way it is the "wrong" action (i.e., it does not work to produce the predicted desired results), it has its positive effects in that it gets a person off dead center. It gives him the image of himself as a person who *can* act, who is more in charge of his own life than he had experienced himself as being when he was in the midst of crisis.

A summary of the steps in this problem-solving is stated succinctly by Hansell: "(1) an energetic inventory of the elements of the predicament, (2) an innovative specification of the options, (3) a precise decision model for selecting among the options, (4) occasions to make and test the decisions, (5) assessing the outcome, and starting over when necessary." [37]

As a part of the decision-making and action-initiating process, the person in crisis must be led to see the *value of personal relationships* and to discover ways of rebuilding those that are in disrepair and methods of establishing those that need to be developed. The frequent occurrence of disturbed, broken, or lost relationships in the onset of crisis makes this emphasis only logical as counselor and counselee in the midst of a meaningful relationship seek to find the resolution of the crisis. Helps to facilitate the person's dealing with relationships are often the new forms of communication that he has learned during the crisis counseling relation.

The step of making an inventory of problem-solving resources with the woman who had come into the church office seemed to be a dry run. She could not report having had precisely these feelings in such a way before. She had, of course, many times felt unhappy and thought that she could not cope with her problems. On these occasions she went to a professional counselor, with much of her adult life being filled with short- and long-term psychotherapy. Since she could identify no other resources, her judgment was that continued psychotherapy was the only option available to her in order to help her function.

Yet, when she and the minister began to discuss what

<hr/>

[37] Norris Hansell, Mary Wodarczyk, and Britomar Handlon-Lathrop, "Decision Counseling Method: Expanding Coping at Crisis-in-Transit," *Archives of General Psychiatry*, XXII (May, 1970), 464-65.

it was that she could do about her present situation, her own feelings seemed to cancel out her only alternative. She had said, "I can never go back to that counselor." Now she was also saying, "I just can't possibly start with a new therapist. It takes so long to establish a relationship. It's so difficult for me to talk to new people. And I'll have to go over so much of the same ground again. I just can't do it." The minister then very clearly stated the dilemma that she had developed for herself, and pointed out that she had developed it: she could not leave his office that day with any sense of self-confidence that she could sustain herself simply with her own inner resources; she did not have family or friends to sustain her; she could not go back to her own counselor; she could not start with a new one. "Do you see where this leaves you? You *must* do one of these. Which one will it be?"

She sat in silence. She could not make the decision. In this instance, with this type of person, one with little ego strength, the minister decided he must evaluate her situation and assist her decision-making in a more direct way than usual procedure would justify. His appraisal was that she needed the continued support of therapy. He also was convinced that it would in fact be easier for her to go back to her former therapist than it would to begin anew. In addition, the former therapist was a part of her problem situation at this time, and the resolution of the crisis would naturally suggest that she work through her feelings *about* him *with* him. Therefore, the minister stated this last point to her, that she had unfinished business with her counselor which it was necessary for her to complete in order to move entirely out of this particular crisis as well as make some solid gains from it. The decision whether to continue with him or to seek a new therapist could be made after that time.

She understood immediately, but was reluctant and somewhat resistant to agreeing that this could become her decision. The minister's procedure was simply to ask her what she *would* do. He repeated her dilemma, did a rerun on the possible outcome and values of each, phrasing much of this in the form of question to which she had to respond, and then stated very firmly as a result that it seemed as if one of the options held more potential value to her as a first step than the others. She agreed, then committed herself to doing it, and the minister confirmed and supported her in it.

A brief summary was made by the minister as to what he understood had been happening in her life recently and what had taken place between the two of them that day, again engaging her in the summary by asking her questions. She made responses that demonstrated her understanding and agreement, and made a restatement of what she was going to do. She left the office after only an hour, no longer in the midst of the crisis with which she had entered. She still had her action to carry out, and she still was a person who carried with her maladaptive behavior patterns from the past. There was no personality reconstruction, no miraculous transformation of the ego. However, the crisis had in one session been effectively resolved, with the promise of at least some modest ego gains and the learning of ways of handling certain aspects of relationships.

In crisis counseling, always built into the last session, or in this instance, the last part of the one session, is the *articulation of the new learning* that has taken place and a discussion of how it might be adapted for coping with possible future crisis. The question is actually raised, "What have you learned from all this?" Reviewing in specific terms what has taken place deposits the material in one's repertoire in such a way that it will be more readily available for future reference, like coding and filing for data storage in a computer. Unsymbolized material is not retrievable and therefore not usable. The counselor in a direct way encourages the person to use what strength he does have to consolidate the gains that have just been made and to utilize his new strength and insight in solving other problems and meeting other crises which will occur in the future. Paul summarizes the process in this way: "In reversing the decompensation and restoring emotional equilibrium, we aim to strengthen the client's resources, to give him not only symptom relief, but also symptom control, social control, and some degree of insight." [38]

Among the guidelines for evaluating the process as it progresses and for moving toward the termination of the counseling relationship in regard to a particular crisis are the following:

Has the level of obvious anxiety decreased significantly?
Can the person describe in his own words a plan of action?
Is he explicitly hopeful regarding the immediate future?
Does he show his appreciation for the help he has received?
Is there a realistic expectation that the unmet needs which
  were related to the crisis itself may now be satisfied in
  some appropriate way? [39]

In viewing the total process of crisis intervention it can readily be seen that both the limitation of time and the steps themselves demand a more active par-

[38] Louis Paul, "Treatment Techniques in a Walk-in Clinic," *Hospital and Community Psychiatry*, XVII (February, 1966), 51.
[39] Rusk, "Opportunity and Technique," 262.

ticipation on the part of the counselor than do the older traditional approaches in which most ministers have been schooled. An active role in questioning, searching, focusing, keeping the person on the present situation, interpreting, giving information, suggesting, calling for decision-making develops naturally in the process. Paul adds the useful suggestion that each session should be conducted as if it were the only opportunity to help the person.[40] For, in fact, many times it is.

SUMMARY

This chapter has sought to present both the goals and the process of crisis counseling. In order to set this process in its proper context, a brief statement was made concerning both the dynamic nature and role of words in any human interaction and those basic ingredients necessary for any helping relationship. Since any counseling is the interaction between persons, it was essential to discuss the minister-counselor as person, taking into consideration his professional role.

In addition to the verbal interpersonal process of crisis counseling as described in detail in this chapter, there are other methodologies of intervention to which reference either was not made or was made only briefly. Several of these fit very closely the pattern of the usual functioning of the minister in his traditional role as pastor as well as some reasonably modern adaptations of the traditional functions. Some of these are frequently necessary and always useful in crisis resolution. These procedures will be discussed in the next chapter.

[40] "Treatment Techniques," 51.

Chapter IV

INTERVENTION PROCEDURES

The previous chapter has described and illustrated with an extended case what crisis counseling looks and sounds like as a process between two persons in a face-to-face setting. There are a number of other strategies of intervention, however, taking a variety of forms. Some of these are frequently essential for minimizing the potential dangers of a crisis and for expediting a successful outcome. Others, while not absolutely necessary, may be quite useful in many instances. The procedures to be discussed in this chapter certainly do not comprise a complete list of the possibilities. To the contrary, a minister is limited in what he does to help people only by his perception of the total situation, which includes the limits of his own creative imagination. In any situation of helping we are never bound by what is standard operating procedure, and should be encouraged to act in any way that might seem to be productive of support and change. The interventions and methodologies to be presented here are among the rather common and important ones and those that also seem to fit quite neatly into the minister's usual pattern of functioning. Some of these are self-evident and need little elaboration; some overlap with others; some will require more detail.

HOME VISITS

The recommendation of the practice of home visitation will sound extremely trite to the minister who is already accustomed to going not only to homes but to offices, places of business, hospitals, and other places where people are found, as a means of his fullest service to them. These visits, as we all know, are made for a number of purposes, including that of individual and family crisis. It is a much more novel idea to other mental health professionals, some of whom are beginning to operate in this fashion with what they believe to be quite valuable results. Such a point does not need to be belabored for ministers, but it is encouraging to realize that a practice which has been standard for us is beginning to be viewed as highly important by others. One mental health professional even declares that it is "essential in crisis intervention as well as in follow-up care." [1] Another demonstrates how it may tie in with the person's need for protection and help and provide the sense of being cared for in a way that the person's coming to the office would not communicate. This writer goes on to warn, however, that the home visit should not be primarily a means of the intervener's filling his own needs and that the immediate dependence that is established in this way should not be encouraged to persist after the peak of the crisis is over.[2] In addition to the positive effect on the rapid establishment of the therapeutic relationship of seeing a person in the setting where he experiences his health and

[1] David Rubenstein, "Rehospitalization Versus Family Crisis Intervention," *American Journal of Psychiatry*, CXXIX (December, 1972), 719.

[2] Beverly Berliner, "Nursing a Patient in Crisis," *American Journal of Nursing*, LXX (October, 1970), 2156.

strength as well as the current situation of distress and sense of helplessness, more actual information may be forthcoming, especially if other family members are there and the counselor can observe their natural interaction with one another.[3] In some crisis intervention clinics a home visit is standard as the first counseling session for some of the reasons mentioned. The minister, then, should never feel that he is somehow less professional because he has gone quickly to the home of the person in distress rather than requiring an appointment with a person in his office. To the contrary, his role as one who is able to move toward people in distress is one of his clear advantages in being immediately helpful to troubled persons.

MOBILIZATION OF INTERPERSONAL RESOURCES

Reference has already been made to the fact that in many instances of crisis other persons are involved in some dynamic way in its development, usually through loss, separation, alienation, disillusionment, the other's failure to meet a person's needs. It has been pointed out that even relatively modest need fulfillment on the part of others is frequently sufficient to exert a significant positive influence on the course of the crisis, and that the repair and renewal of relationships may be an important part of crisis resolution. Often, however, the positive potentialities of other people are not as readily available to the person in crisis in ordinary everyday transactions as they might be if attention to their respon-

---

[3] Frank S. Pittman, Carol DeYoung, Kalman Flomenhaft, David M. Kaplan, and Donald G. Longsley. "Crisis Family Therapy." *Current Psychiatric Therapies*, VI, Jules H. Masserman, ed. (New York: Grune & Stratton, 1966), p. 190.

sibilities and possible helping roles were focused by someone who is seen as more objective and also recognized and respected as an expert or an authority. Therefore, "convening key people of the troubled person's social network into the background of the counseling relationship can sometimes greatly increase its innovative power." [4]

Two factors may be at work in crisis: the real or perceived withdrawal of interpersonal need satisfactions and/or the person's own withdrawal or the adoption of behavior which alienates others from him. In any instance, he needs the understanding and support of others in his social system, and while in some crises this may come rather naturally and easily, in others there may be resistances to helping. It then becomes important for these others as well as the person in crisis to understand his real needs and the meaning of his tendencies to isolate himself or to push others away from him in anger or fear or disgust or some combination of these. Only in such understanding will many people be able to overcome the barriers to sharing concern and to helpful behavior.

Therefore, the counselor may actually take the initiative to call together in a group setting members of the family, employer and coworkers, friends, a young person's teachers, others who seem to be related to him— sometimes with and sometimes without the person— for evaluating the situation. The aim is to enable them to see how they may be helpful, to point out their responsibilities, deal with their feelings about the person and their role in his life, develop options, make decisions. The specific persons who are called together, of course, vary with the situation. No pattern is followed

[4] Hansell, "Decision Counseling Method," p. 464.

rigidly in every case. The mobilizing of other persons is always done with the knowledge, and hopefully the consent, of the person in crisis. The program for bringing others into the situation develops as a result of discussing with the distressed person all the issues involved, the relationship of these others to him, their positive and/or negative roles in the crisis, and the importance of bringing them into the picture. Many times the person will be relieved that someone is taking the initiative to assist in bringing him into significant contact with these others. On occasion, of course, a person may be anxious, reluctant, or even resistant to such a meeting. His reasons and his feelings should be listened to with understanding and respect, and you may in fact change your mind about following through on this course of action. If, however, you are absolutely convinced of its importance, you must communicate this very strongly to the person, and in severe crisis insist on it, even though he refuses to cooperate. It must be made clear that he has asked you to act in his best interests and that you are now doing so. (Obviously, the force of this point is lost if you have yourself taken the initiative to go to the person in crisis.) Nevertheless, it is essential that you communicate your conviction about what ought to be done. This is especially important in a suicidal crisis or where there seems to be the danger of a psychotic break.

In addition to obtaining more data about the person from another perspective, this process confirms to the distressed person the existence of resources which he may have blocked out or distorted.

It is obvious that on occasion the appropriate persons to call together are the family. Again, a family is often quite responsive, and the members are open to discussing how they may help and are quite relieved that some-one is assisting them as well as the person in crisis. Occasionally there may be resistance, but the counselor should be quite direct in pointing out their respon-sibility for one of their own family members. The min-ister should keep in mind that all references to individ-uals and their crises hold true for the family context for the crisis. To be specific, this means that crises may take place in both healthy and unhealthy family systems. Obviously the former are easier to work with in terms of their responsiveness and openness to expected con-structive results in a shorter period of time. Yet just as no individual is 100 percent ill, no family is either, and Rubenstein has pointed out that even if the family system is basically a destructive one, it may still be seen as a potential resource for the person in crisis in regard to the resolution of this present reaction.[5] What the family may offer in regard to support in the present crisis must be clearly distinguished from what they offer in terms of possibilities for a radical change of per-sonality or life-style. Some care, some understanding, some active support for a family member may be found in almost any family. It is such family strength that the counselor may need to search for at this time. Rusk indicates that a family may either overestimate its own destructiveness or underestimate its compe-tence.[6] The minister may help them get a somewhat more balanced view of themselves and discover what resources they do have, even though these may admit-tedly be minimal.

If the family system is not basically a sound one, the minister must take great care to continue to focus only

[5] "Rehospitalization Versus Family Crisis Intervention," p. 719.
[6] "Opportunity and Technique," p. 259.

on what they need at this time to help a member with this crisis. As in an individual, the temptation to pursue other and long-standing problems must be resisted. Even if the family has other serious needs, any discussion of these and the possible modification of the destructive elements of the system must wait until *this present crisis* is taken care of. However, the impact of the crisis upon the family and their discovery that some positive strengths have been mobilized to meet a member's needs might provide an initial motivation for further whole family help.[7]

MANIPULATION OF COUNSELING TIME

Many ministers have been quite impressed with one of the practices of the psychotherapist, specifically that of seeing persons in hour-long sessions once a week, without realizing that many therapists themselves have different standard patterns and most utilize considerable flexibility of schedule, depending upon the person's needs, the stage of therapy, and other factors. Crisis is one of those situations where one hour per week of face-to-face counseling may or may not be appropriate.

The minister should learn to follow his own sense of the situation with complete flexibility to meet most effectively the particular needs of this one unique person at this time. Recognizing that the minister is an extremely busy person, he still operates within a schedule that has more possible flexibility than many other professionals. This advantage is pointed out in a most

[7] Rubenstein, "Rehospitalization Versus Family Crisis Intervention," p. 718.

emphatic way by a prominent mental health practitioner and teacher:

We have been impressed in the consultation groups by the number of ministers who report not only answering an anguished phone call with a home visit within a short time, but also with the way in which, after assessing the situation, they can spend two, three, or even five hours containing a threatened explosion. After such intensive and prompt infusions of support, it is instructive to note how quickly a parishioner returns to independence and a normal functioning; whereas denying him such lavish help in a crisis often creates a need for long-term care.[8]

In addition to assigning a large block of time to an immediate emergency, the crisis counselor may decide after the first session to have another just two or three days in the future rather than waiting for the sacred number of seven. He may have two interviews a week for the first two or three weeks, then stop entirely, or reduce them to one per week. The time of termination may be judged by using the criteria listed for evaluating the success of crisis counseling (p. 100), and by explicitly discussing with the person whether he has reached the point where he feels that he can make it without the counselor.

The decision of closer spacing than once a week may be judged by the intensity of anxiety or confusion or sense of unreality remaining after the first interview, by the presence of suicidal communication, and by the presence of identified external stress during the coming days. If the level of anxiety or other central affective symptoms have not seemed to be reduced during the

[8] Ruth B. Caplan, *Helping the Helpers to Help* (New York: Seabury Press, 1972), p. 20.

first interview, or if reduced, they still seem to be at a highly painful or incapacitating level, then another session would seem to be called for within a shorter interval than usual.

Certainly where there are explicit or implicit suicidal communications, it would be important to put another meeting on the schedule within two or three days. The feeling that there is no future is a part of the suicidal person's perception of himself in his world, and to create such a future is the immediate task of all persons in his life. After a reasonably good session, a specific date only a short time hence performs the function of making a gift of at least that much future and is a breakthrough. Explicit suicidal language is self-evident. "I am thinking about killing myself." Implicit suicidal language can be recognized in the following statements: "I just don't see how I can stand all this much longer." "There's no use trying to go on." "My family would really be better off without me." "There's actually no meaning at all to life, is there?" While people may use both explicit and implicit suicidal language and not be highly lethal, it is the responsibility of the minister to check this out carefully, making the implicit explicit, examining its meaning, talking with the person about it in plain language. It is reason enough not to wait a week for the next interview to check it out further.

Another guideline for scheduling the date of the next session is the determination of continued or additional situational stress during the days immediately following. Is there going to be a medical report with some probability of bad news? Are all the children going to be home from school an added two days? Is there to be a critical interview with the boss? Might someone close to the person be dying? If so, schedule a session at the most opportune time.

In summary, read the person and the situation sensitively, discuss the issues with him, be flexible, do what needs to be done as you examine the total situation. And remember, in crisis it will do no harm to schedule the next visit only two or three days later; it will usually be helpful and may sometimes make a critical difference in sustaining a person and turning the direction of the crisis around. The greater mistake would be to wait too long for the next time together.

THE USE OF THE TELEPHONE

Everyone uses the telephone, and everyone knows how to use it. So why say, "Use the telephone." Yet in the context of the strategy of intervention in crisis, the active and creative use of this instrument of communication is often overlooked and the differences between face-to-face and telephone counseling are frequently ignored.

When to Use the Telephone

Even with the increase in the amount of pastoral care and counseling being taught in seminary, the broadening scope and the depth of the teaching, and an increase in nonclassroom training opportunities, very little is being done to educate students in the effective use of the telephone as a pastoral care and counseling medium. There are a few exceptions to this statement, to be sure, such as the course in crisis intervention offered by Perkins School of Theology, where, after initial preparatory training, students actually become volunteers at the Suicide Prevention Center or at Contact, a church-related agency, both of which use the telephones exclusively for their service. There are continued weekly supervisory sessions for the remainder of the nine-month academic year.

Just as little is being taught in the seminaries, a review of the professional psychotherapeutic literature reveals no more than a handful of articles which deal with the subject of the telephone in therapy. The upshot of all this is that in the face of the frequent use of the phone by the minister and some increasing use of it by other professionals as a therapeutic tool, there is a dearth of literature and very little education in regard to a reinforcement of its importance and very few clues to its appropriate and most effective utilization. By this oversight and neglect, the implication must be that it is not important to use the telephone and that when one does it is either like any other counseling session or like any other conversation. This is a false communication.

Every minister knows that very frequently people in crisis will make their first contact with him by phone. If the minister is not in a position to go immediately to the person, usually the preferred response, and the person cannot come very soon to the church office or the parsonage, the first session itself may take place right at that time by phone, whether it lasts only ten or fifteen minutes or an hour or more. Indeed, for a few people, because of their desire to remain anonymous or for other reasons, all the counseling they receive will be by phone.

Even when face-to-face interviews are scheduled, the phone should be used in at least three other sets of circumstances. First, there should almost always be some follow-up by the minister and "checking in" by the troubled person, especially in the early stages of the intervention process, with this procedure being explained by the minister and explicitly agreed to by the person. The rationale for this strategy will be explained in the next section.

Second, the person in crisis should feel free to call the minister between appointments for brief talks in case of emergency, when his anxiety level rises sharply or other affective symptoms reach a frightening or seemingly hopeless point. These calls may appropriately be only a few minutes in length, although some may need to be longer. In this specific situation, the call is not considered to be a substitute for an appointment. For example, the person may be coming in the very next day, but during the afternoon or evening feels an intense inner pressure that is either unbearably painful or in the midst of which he feels as if he may lose control. It is possible that only five or ten minutes of expressing his feelings on the phone to the minister, hearing the minister's voice and sensing his care, reestablishing contact with reality through the relationship that is communicated voice to voice, will be sufficient to sustain the person until the appointment the next day.

The minister and the person receiving help should use the phone for the regular appointment if for some reason, such as illness, the counselee is unable to come to the church, and it is impractical for the minister to go to him.

The effectiveness of the telephone as a point of contact has now been proved beyond all doubt through the experience of dozens of suicide prevention and crisis intervention centers across this country, in Europe, Australia, and in other parts of the world. In addition, other mental health clinics have begun to use it to supplement other phases of their therapy with patients.[9]

Rosenblum raises the point that while some people may be able to tolerate the pressure of a close face-to-face relationship, others may be so threatened by a personal visit that the contact may be more effectively maintained by phone. Therefore, if the caller is a person with whom the minister does not already have an established relationship, while it is certainly appropriate that the minister suggest that he visit in the home or that the caller come to the office, he should not be so insistent as to close off his usefulness by means of the phone. Rosenblum stresses that some persons may be overwhelmed by sustained personal contact, but at the same time are seeking some personal sustenance. The availability of voice contact is supremely important for them, for their own ventilation, for reassurance, to sustain the image that someone is there who cares. He concludes: "Telephone therapy deserves a legitimate place in the armamentorium of the therapist and the clinic. It should not be accorded second class status. It can serve as a useful adjunct to the more orthodox therapies." [10]

Differences Between Telephone and Face-to-Face Counseling

There are certain obvious differences between a counseling session conducted on the telephone and one at which the persons are physically present with one another, yet our awareness of these differences has not always led us to the conscious development of those dis-

[9] Ronald J. Catanzaro, "WATS Telephone Therapy: New Follow-up Technique for Alcoholics," *American Journal of Psychiatry*, CXVI (January, 1970), 1024-27; A. J. R. Koumans, J. J. Muller, and C. F. Miller, "Use of Telephone Calls to Increase Motivation," *Psychological Reports*, XXI (1967), 327-28.

[10] Lewis Rosenblum, "Telephone Therapy," *Psychotherapy: Theory, Research, and Practice*, VI (Fall, 1969), 241, 242.

ciplined practices that would make us more effective.

One of the major differences, of course, has to do with the fact that our usual perception and modes of communication with people include the physical. In a group when a person speaks, it is almost automatic that we turn to look at him as we are listening. We are seldom consciously aware that what we then hear is both added to and taken away from by what we see. It is only when we cannot bring another person into our field of vision that we realize the sum total of the cues that are missing: the way a person cares for himself physically, his posture, what the hands and eyes are doing, tenseness versus relaxation, reddening of the neck, cheeks, and around the eyes, tears, a smile or a frown, bodily movement, palpitation of the neck indicating stronger and more rapid heart beat, all these and others are no longer there for us to see and interpret. And while these are of great significance when they accompany the words of another person, they are perhaps even more important for us to observe while we ourselves are speaking and during times of complete silence.

The lack of visual stimuli requires much more sensitive and perceptive listening on the part of the counselor. He must be much more aware of the meaning of the tone of the voice, its tremors and cracking, changes in volume and pitch, modulation, hesitation, quantity, and pace of verbal production, the timing and length of the pauses, sighing, choking, and other sounds, especially as these may be revelatory of feelings on the part of the caller. It may often necessitate the type of comment or specific questions that one would not typically ask in face-to-face contact because their answers would be apparent if the counselor could see the person. For example, "It sounds as if you are crying at this time." Or, "It's difficult for me to decide whether you are laughing or crying." Or, "It seems as if your voice is higher than it was earlier. I wonder what you are feeling right now."

At the same time, the counselor must be just as aware that the person on the other end of the line lacks visual perception of him. The physical stimuli are not available for the person in crisis either. This demands more verbal participation by the counselor. He must confirm his meaningful presence through sound, whereas in a face-to-face setting the same things might be communicated through nodding, eye contact, a gesture of the hand, and other nonverbal signals that communicate that he is there and attentive.

The minister's use of his voice as a means of establishing relationship quickly and easily without the visual stimuli is even more crucial in telephone crisis intervention than in preaching or the usual pastoral care and counseling situations, although they are obviously of great importance there. The quality of the voice makes a great difference—whether it is flat and monotone or alive and flexible, whiney and shrill or well-rounded, too loud or too soft. Changes of the voice communicate a variety of feelings, including warmth and caring and assurance. In addition, on the telephone it becomes more appropriate to express concern through explicit words as well as through the tone of voice. The importance of the confirmation of presence also requires that silences on the phone should not last as long as they might when persons are physically present with each other. This should not be interpreted to mean either that the counselor seeks to force the other to talk or that he merely chatters away at something so there will not be silence. Rather, after a brief period, he may ask, "What feelings are you having during the silence?" Or if it is obvious that the emotion is extremely powerful, he may reflect, "When you feel very intensely about something, it's often quite difficult to express it in words." Or occasionally when there is no response to questions or statements like the above, simply, "I'm still here with you."

Another difference between telephone and face-to-face counseling is that the other person has much more control over the termination of the session. Often enough in counseling a person's frustration and anger or fright or other feelings lead to the desire to reject or escape from the counselor and the situation. Nevertheless, when they are together in the same room, social inhibitions usually exercise pressure on the person to continue to sit there even when he would prefer to leave. This provides the opportunity for the counselor to perceive the feelings and to facilitate their expression and working through. On the phone there are far fewer social restraints, and it is much easier for the person to hang up. The telephone counselor must be aware of the dynamics of this situation, pay close attention to rising frustration, anger, fear, encourage the person actively to express these, and be willing to function in a situation where he gives up some authority and control to the person in need.

The Need for Discipline

One very experienced professional in the practice and supervision of telephone crisis intervention points out one of the dangers of the method. Because of our customary social conversational use of the phone, it is easy to allow the disciplines of crisis counseling to grow lax and the verbal transaction to deteriorate into nothing but conversation. Undisciplined chitchat about crucially significant matters is still nothing but chitchat and is just not therapeutic. The conversational model of transaction on the phone, he believes, is worse than nothing at all when talking with a person in crisis.[11] Therefore, when moving from face-to-face counseling to telephone intervention, the counselor must be consciously aware of the change of modality and deliberately call into play his most disciplined methods of listening and responding. The situation demands that the concentration be intense.

FOLLOW-UP: RATIONALE AND PROCEDURES

It should now be clear that a major contribution to the life of a person in crisis is another person who genuinely cares, who seeks to understand and help him understand, who brings a perspective on the problem area that is broader and more realistic than that of the distressed person with his narrowed focus of attention, who offers hope. Also, the more severe the crisis, the less hope, the less future the person experiences. Therefore, any activities that make for more frequent contact between the helping person and the person in crisis will support those goals implied by the statement of needs that has just been made. The closer spacing of interviews and emergency telephone calls at the initiative of the person experiencing stress have already been discussed.

The follow-up may take two directions. First, the minister will call back on the phone or will go by to

[11] Gene W. Brockopp, "The Telephone Call—Conversation or Therapy," *Crisis Intervention*, II (1970), 73.

see the person, the latter's often being preferable and even practical from the minister's point of view. However, if a visit to the home, office, or hospital is not practical, then the phone is an extremely convenient instrument to use. Obviously when the minister is in an extremely busy period, he can usually make several phone calls in the time it may take him to go to a home a number of miles away. The call may be specifically scheduled and agreed to, or it may come spontaneously out of the minister's immediate caring, wondering how the person is, what is going on. The second direction is from the person in crisis to the minister, not only in emergency, but as a result of a commitment to call following some particular action or some period of time.

For example, one outcome of a counseling session might be agreement that the person go to the family doctor or to a particular agency, or tell a spouse or parents about his present feelings and that he is seeing someone about the crisis. The agreement is made that this will take place within two days and that on the third day the person will report back or the minister will call. In the afternoon of the second day, however, the minister, remembering how anxious the person was about doing it, or that the person was still quite depressed when he left the office, or simply having the person very much on his mind, picks up the phone, calls, and says, "I was just thinking about you. You were hurting so much the other day. I was wondering how you feel right now and how things are going with you."

Values of Follow-up

These procedures accomplish several purposes, and several dynamics are operating at the same time. First, the minister's going by to see the person or calling him on the phone confirms his caring. A therapist in a secular setting which has been using the telephone as a follow-up support for alcoholics, states their experience: "The fact that the therapist, not the patient, usually initiates the phone call helps indicate to the patient that the therapist is actively interested in his welfare and is not just a passive participant." [12] This sense that someone genuinely cares is a potent force in supporting the ego strength of the distressed person.

Second, and an alternative strategy, obtaining a commitment from the troubled person to check back in supports the expectation that he must take responsibility for his own life and must take certain initiatives in the helping process. Additionally, when he actually does do this, the act itself is ego-strengthening.

Third, the commitment to check with each other at a specific time gives the person that much future, something positive to look forward to that he may not have had before. As mentioned earlier, this is an absolute necessity for the person with strong suicidal thoughts and feelings.

Fourth, along the same line, the frequency of contacts, the expression of caring, the doing something for oneself, the creation of even a short-term future, all create and encourage hope in the midst of crisis, the hope that action can be taken and things can change.

Fifth, follow-up calls allow for further catharsis.

Sixth, the knowledge on the part of the person in crisis that there definitely will be a follow-up call is an impetus to act upon the decisions that have been made and to pursue agreed upon goals.

Seventh, the procedure provides a means of evaluat-

[12] Catanzaro, "WATS Telephone Therapy," p. 1026.

ing results of action taken, producing the feedback necessary for further decision-making.

REFERRAL AND TRANSFERRAL

The word "referral" is common enough in our usage and in our actual practice of suggesting that the person seeing us about some personal problem or difficult situation see someone else instead, or in addition, in order that their needs might be more fully and effectively met. No minister is so out of touch with reality that he believes that he alone can meet all the needs of all persons. Our very best service to many people is to assist them in getting to others who specialize in those areas of service where the person's needs are. Clinebell states that "properly conceived, referral is a means of using a team effort to help a troubled person. It is a *broadening* and *sharing*, not total *transfer* of responsibility. It employs the division-of-labor principal that is the basis of interprofessional cooperation." [13]

When a minister is working with a person in crisis, it would seldom if ever mean that the minister is merely shifting the person to some other professional or agency and then stepping completely out of the picture. Most often he will remain the primary crisis counselor, as secondary referrals are made for needs that he cannot possibly fill: medical examination, treatment, and prescription, child care agencies, employment agencies, and many others. Even in those situations where a psychiatrist or psychologist might become a primary therapist for a few weeks, the minister should properly remain actively engaged with the person as a caring and sup-

[13] Howard Clinebell, *Basic Types of Pastoral Counseling* (Nashville: Abingdon Press, 1966), p. 177.

porting friend, as a representative of the community of faith, and the primary professional in follow-up support and counseling after the crisis is effectively resolved with the psychiatrist or psychologist.

Referral is used when it is determined that there are relevant needs of the person in crisis that cannot be met by the minister himself. The appropriate professional or agency or organization is then recommended as a part of the total therapeutic plan. The initiative is usually left up to the person in crisis to make his own arrangements, although in some instances the way may be made easier by advance calls from the clergyman. There is, of course, the follow-up procedure mentioned earlier which encourages and supports the person's initiative.

The term "transferral" is used to refer to occasions of severe crisis when a person is seen to be a danger to himself or someone else or is on the verge of a psychotic reaction. Not only is seeing someone else recommended, but the crisis counselor takes whatever steps are necessary to get him there and does not relinquish his primary responsibility with the person until the other professional or agency clearly assumes it. In severe crisis, one does not suggest a referral, then simply wait several days before determining whether the person has gone. It may then be too late.

When to Refer or Transfer

The decision to refer or transfer is determined by the needs of the person that are relevant to the crisis and the ability of the minister to meet those needs. When he cannot, someone else must be found who can. In many of these instances, as suggested earlier, the minister will remain the primary crisis counselor who is

coordinating the total plan. He will need to know, however, when to relinquish his primary role to someone
else and shift into a supportive and follow-up role
only. It should be reemphasized that this is not a cop-
out, nor does it suggest that the secondary and supportive function is not important. Quite to the contrary,
both the referral and the continued pastoral relationship may be absolutely crucial to a successful outcome.

To repeat, transferral is indicated when there seems
to be a serious threat of violence against someone else,
when the person is a high suicide risk, or his behavior
is reaching psychotic proportions, that is, his grasp on
reality is being lost, and he is becoming mentally or
emotionally unavailable to the type of counseling which
the minister can do.

Referral is in order when mood and emotional and
behavioral changes are apparent, but a precipitating
event cannot be discovered within two or three sessions.
Or if the precipitating event be identified and the
symptoms remain severe (that is, a high level of anxiety,
deep depression, extreme confusion, inability to do anything) after five or six sessions, particularly if the period
of time from the precipitating event to the fifth or sixth
session is six weeks or more, this is sufficient evidence
that the usual crisis intervention procedures are not
being effective. Many would also want to refer when
after two or three sessions it is discovered that in addition to the symptoms of the crisis, there is long-term
underlying pathology. Some well-trained ministers may
be able to separate the crisis symptoms from the earlier
symptoms and work effectively with the person on the
crisis, but it may become quite complex.

One illustration may show some of the extreme needs
of a person with reasonably few ego strengths when there

123

is also a crisis reaction. A seventeen-year-old girl had made a mild suicide attempt and was brought to a minister by her employer. She was very depressed and felt she had nothing to live for. She had had periods of depression before and one previous mild suicide attempt. The precipitating event for this particular extreme feeling of worthlessness and hopelessness had been a violent argument with her mother. The home background was extremely bad and the present home situation poor. The girl had dropped out of school, already had a serious drinking problem, and was sexually promiscuous. Even though her present depression fit the definition of crisis, her whole background and pattern of maladaptive and self-destructive behavior were so bad, and the present depression so severe as to prevent her being sufficiently available for counseling, and the minister raised directly the question of how it might be possible for her to handle her life in the near future. She felt totally without strength, and could not promise not to try to kill herself. The minister suggested the hospital as a place where she would be completely taken care of for a short period of time and would not have to assume responsibility for herself, which right at the moment she felt incapable of doing. She agreed that she would like to be cared for in this way until she could do more for herself. The minister called the hospital, arranged for the admission procedure, told the girl's employer and asked him to take her and to call the mother to meet them and sign the admission papers. The minister the next day called the administrative psychiatrist and discussed the situation with him. When the girl was discharged after a week, much of the depression gone, he began a counseling relationship with her.

Certainly some people overdramatize their problems, both in the degree of suicidal feelings they report or in their underestimation of their own strength. Nevertheless, when the minister has discussed these issues in a direct way with a person and has some sense that person is reporting himself accurately, it is better to believe the self-description and take the necessary transferral steps than it is to make what might be a disastrous misjudgment in the other direction.

Naturally, referral should also always be considered after a crisis is resolved if the person has other problems he would like to work on but which are either beyond the limits of the minister's own training and experience or for which he does not have sufficient time.

Methods of Referral

The final issue is *how* a referral or transferral should be made. The first and obvious necessity, once a person's needs have been clearly determined, is to refer to the appropriate professionals and agencies, those that are clearly designed to meet the specific identified needs. This will require a rather full knowledge of community resources, or at least where, with one or two phone calls, the proper ones may be found. It should also include at least some personal knowledge of professionals, both in private practice and those who work for a variety of agencies. Referral to a place where the person's identified needs cannot be met is a particularly frustrating experience, and additional frustration, disappointment, and anger is precisely what the person in crisis does not need at this time. It can actually speed the deterioration of the situation in many instances. We must know what the professionals or agencies offer.

Second, the need for referral should be presented to the person in crisis in a sensitive and reassuring manner. The need which has to be met, the reasons why the pastor himself cannot meet it adequately, and the appropriateness of the particular person or agency being suggested should all be cogently explained in detail.

Third, the person should have the opportunity to express his feelings in response to the referral or transferral suggestion. These feelings should be accepted as genuine, and there should be understanding of some of the real difficulties the person may have emotionally in following through on the suggestion and of the actual inconvenience which may be involved.

Fourth, if, however, it is clear to the minister that legitimate needs have been identified, that they are related to the crisis, and that they can be met more adequately somewhere else, a summary of this is made in as convincing a manner as the minister can do it. The person in crisis must not be allowed to play the "please help me but I won't let you" game by refusing to accept and act on suggestions that would facilitate the resolution of the crisis.

Fifth, the minister should reassure the person in crisis of his deep concern and verify the fact that the referral or transferral does not mean that the minister will step out of his life. Many people are sensitive to any signal that the helping person might be rejecting them. No matter how well the need for referral is explained in a rational manner, some people still experience it as rejection. The minister might need to verbalize this for the person in crisis in order to assist him to express his genuine feelings and be able to work these through: "Now I know that in suggesting that you go see the psychiatrist, some people would feel that I didn't want to work with them myself. I wonder if you are having some of these feelings right now." The minister should encourage the expression of whatever feelings of rejection or anger that the person might be having, then clarify in detail that their relationship will continue, that he will continue to be the primary counselor, or if not this, he will be in touch regularly with the person to see how things are going and to help in any way he can.

Finally, be sure to follow up on the referrals or transferrals with the person to see if appointments were made and kept and what the results were and what the next steps should be.

Clinebell lists a number of guidelines for effective referral procedures. While not all of them are applicable to the referral of the person in crisis, they are of value and the minister should familiarize himself with them.[14]

CRISIS COUNSELING IN GROUPS

The placing of persons in crisis into a small group as a new modality for helping them more effectively in their distress has been described by several professionals working in the setting of crisis intervention centers and hospitals. While probably impossible in small churches and communities, and impractical in some of moderate size, it would seem to hold great promise for the minister in larger churches and in the city. It could afford some saving of the minister's own time and greater aid for those with whom he is working. Even those ministers who feel at this time that the approach is not for them should seek to understand the procedure, evalu-

[14] *Ibid.*, pp. 182-86.

ate it fairly, and be alert for those opportunities that might present themselves at a later date.

Values of the Group Approach

The group method is particularly recommended to those ministers who are serving in poverty and minority areas and who are not themselves members of that particular class or racial or ethnic group. One of the difficulties encountered in a variety of forms in a traditional ministry to lower socio-economic classes, and especially to Blacks and Mexican Americans, by those who are Anglo-Saxon and middle-class or above has not usually been a lack of commitment and desire, but a massive lack of understanding, an inability to get inside the experience of the other, a failure to grasp structures of thought, and quite simply a different language. Many of these handicaps can be overcome when much of the personal understanding, the offering of alternatives of coping behavior, assistance with decision-making, and support of the new behavior comes from an individual's own peers in a group.[15]

Confirmation of the value of crisis groups has come from two studies. One of these was in a hospital setting where immediate hospitalization was not indicated, but where individual treatment was not available for six weeks. A pilot study showed that over 50 percent of the patients were definitely improved as a result of being placed immediately in a group which met for a six-week period. This led the professionals to a decision to carry on a more intensive examination of the pro-

[15] Jean M. Allgeyer, "The Crisis Group: Its Unique Usefulness to the Disadvantaged," *International Journal of Group Psychotherapy*, XX (April, 1970), 235-40.

cedure. Patients were placed in groups meeting one and a half hours each week, with up to ten persons in each group, each person attending a maximum of six sessions. New persons could come into a group at any time. Seventy-eight patients were in the experimental groups and ninety patients were in a control group receiving traditional forms of psychotherapy. At the conclusion of the study, the therapists had spent in terms of their own time an average of one and a half hours per individual in the experimental group and eight and a half hours per individual in the control group. In a six-month follow-up, 83 percent of the experimental group reported continued improvement, over twice as many as those receiving the usual individual treatment. The obvious conclusion was that the group method was a time-saver and was clearly more helpful.[16]

A study in a crisis intervention setting designed three levels of assessment of outcome, with sixteen out of the thirty clients showing maximum improvement, and nine others showing minimal or moderate improvement.[17] While this investigation does indicate that people are definitely helped by the crisis group, the report unfortunately included no reference to a control group receiving individual counseling, so no comparative judgment can be made.

Description of the Procedure

The first and obvious practical difficulty in beginning a crisis intervention group in the context of the

[16] Demetrius A. Trakas and Gertrude Lloyd, "Emergency Management in a Short-term Open Group," *Comprehensive Psychiatry*, XII (March, 1971), 170-74.
[17] Martin Strickler and Jean Allgeyer, "The Crisis Group: A New Application of Crisis Theory," *Social Work*, XII (July, 1967), 32.

local church is to have available during a single week at least four people in the early stages of crisis who respond positively to the minister's suggestion that they meet together for several sessions. The other problem is that of sustaining the group with a minimum of four persons over an extended period of time, requiring that the church and/or community setting be large enough so that new persons are constantly available to come into it.

If a group is feasible from this standpoint, however, the procedures of the Benjamin Rush Clinic in Los Angeles seem directly adaptable to the minister's work. An article by Morley and Brown presents their procedures quite clearly and in detail.[18] Every person who comes into the clinic is seen individually for the first session. At this time it is determined whether the person is in crisis. If so, a specific formulation of the crisis situation is made, the precipitating event identified, the threat explored, previous and potential coping mechanisms surveyed, and preparation is made for the person to enter the group. While in their practice there are certain guidelines relating to language difficulty or to other psychiatric problems which would exclude a person from the group setting, it is not necessary to seek to have a homogeneous group, that is, all one sex, marital status, age. In the person's first group session, he begins by telling the others what led him to seek help and summarizes what he has discovered during the first session about himself and his crisis reaction. The group counselor assists him in elaborating the meaning

[18] Wilbur Morley and Vivian B. Brown, "The Crisis-Intervention Group: A Natural Mating or a Marriage of Convenience?" *Psychotherapy: Theory, Research, and Practice,* VI (Winter, 1969),30-36. The section heading outline which follows is theirs.

of the precipitating event, the form of the crisis, and the previous attempts at coping which have failed. Two or even three persons might be able to introduce themselves to a group in this way in the first session. The counselor facilitates the group in helping the person to express his feelings, to explore alternative coping mechanisms and courses of action which might help change the person or the situation, and encourages mutual support. As in individual crisis counseling, the group leader also directly discourages the discussion of chronic problems, explains why certain behavior which is an attempt to deal with the feelings and situation is destructive and rejects consideration of this. Every person understands that he is to have a maximum of five group sessions and that his work must be done in this period of time.

Differences from Usual Therapy Groups

There are a number of differences between crisis intervention groups and most usual therapy groups, obviously a function of the nature of crisis and its inherent time limits.

First, there is not a focus on the deep development of the group as a group, with a major concern on the analysis of the group process. Rather, there is much more attention given to the individual by both the counselor and the group, with group support and stimulation. This focus is designed to meet the peculiar needs of the person in crisis. It should also be obvious that the development of group feeling in the usual therapy sense would be made extremely difficult by the fact that a person is in the group for no more than five sessions and the fact that persons are leaving it constantly and new ones entering. Even so it has been the experience of those who have been involved in crisis groups that because of the intense emotions of crisis and the need for psychosocial support, rapport and a sense of empathy are rapidly established between group members.

Second, time is of the essence. No person in the group can be allowed to sit quietly until he feels like participating verbally. Those who are most verbal cannot be allowed to dominate. There is much more calling on people to respond, much more going around the entire group so that every member may express himself on an issue or respond with his feelings.

Third, as the first two obviously would require, the group leader is extremely active. Of course, this is true of some counselors in other groups, but it is an absolute requirement in a crisis group in order to accomplish the goals of crisis resolution in a short period of time and to maintain the process just referred to.

Differences from Individual Crisis Counseling

There are also differences, primarily in the direction of advantages, between group and individual crisis counseling. First, there is the value of group support. There can be a genuine and important offering of help, caring, and hope, both inside and outside the group to a degree that no individual counselor alone could afford. Significant social relationships may grow out of the group association, providing sustenance between group sessions and continuing help after an individual's formal counseling is at an end.

Second, since the feelings of each member are so close to the surface, there seems to be a mutual stimulation to express feelings openly. This may be done often by words themselves, but most of the time it is simply by being in the presence of those who are expressing their emotions. There may also often be similarities of affect that touch quite deeply those who share them, leading to a depth of affective expression and exploration which might have been more difficult under other circumstances. Some persons may also be desensitized, that is, certain types of situations or relationships or events which are highly charged emotionally in their own lives and which cause them distress may become less painful or threatening by these same matters' being discussed over and over again by others.

Third, the way an individual functions in a group often reveals the type of faulty response to persons or situations that is very much a part of his present problem. The counselor is alert to these styles of relating, makes certain the group is aware of what the person is doing, and asks the other members to respond to this behavior and discuss other ways he might handle himself in relation to others.[19]

Finally, there is in a group additional input for alternative coping mechanisms and feedback on decision-making. No matter how intelligent and creative the counselor may be, it is self-evident that several people can think of more things and provide a greater variety of feedback than just one. Often these suggestions and positive and negative criticisms might be accepted more readily by a person from peers who are undergoing crisis than they would be from the professional.

Difficulties of Group Crisis Counseling

One of the major difficulties in group crisis counseling is the additional burden on the counselor to be

[19] Strickler, "The Crisis Group," p. 31.

fully aware at all times of all the needs of the individuals and also the necessities of the group process. It is not easy to keep a focus on the crisis of *every individual* in the group, especially while several members are responding to the crisis of one. Yet no one's crisis must ever be lost from the counselor's attention. In the second place, the first crisis which a person presents may, upon further investigation, turn out not to be the primary or most potent one. A crisis covered by another crisis is more difficult to identify in a group setting where the demands on the counselor's attention are so great. Finally, the counselor must be much more alert to potentially destructive coping behavior which is suggested by members of the group. He must hear and evaluate quickly, ask for feedback by other members, explain the potential destructiveness and why it cannot be allowed, and use this situation as effective teaching, not only for the person to whom the suggestion was directed but also for the person or persons making it and for the group as a whole.

It is clear, in spite of these difficulties, that where the formation of a crisis group is feasible in terms of the number of persons available to start and continue it, it is a method of preference in helping the persons significantly in a brief period of time.

CONCLUSION

This chapter has sought to present some of the important and sometimes essential intervention procedures for assisting persons toward the resolution of their crises. Many of these are methods which many clergy are already utilizing, combining in some form a number of the traditional pastoral functions, their genuine concern for persons, some procedures borrowed from other professionals which seem appropriate to the minister's own functioning, and their own creativity.

Probably the final emphasis of this discussion should be on the matter of the minister's creative imagination in developing a program of help, styled for a particular person with his particular problem in his particular life context. The pastoral counselor should be free to use flexibly in a manner appropriate to the unique situation which every person in crisis provides, the means and procedures of helping that are available. Any creative impulses to respond to the person's need in ways which are not among the standard procedures should not be inhibited initially just because they are new. They should be encouraged to spring fully forth into consciousness, and only then tested to see if they are within the bounds of what the minister understands the goals of crisis counseling to be and within the disciplines of the total procedure as previously outlined in chapter 3. If they are judged to be potentially helpful, then they should be attempted.

The minister should never forget that he has available for many people the valuable resources of the community of faith as a whole community, its various subgroups and programs and activities, its individual members, the faith itself, the authority of his ministerial office, the tendency of many persons both inside and outside the church (although obviously not all, and he should certainly be prepared for this) to respond to his initiative with them in his attempt to be helpful. He should be imaginative in the use of these and other resources in the service of persons who are suffering emotionally.

Chapter V

THE MINISTER'S ROLE AND FUNCTIONING IN THE CRISIS OF GRIEF

It would be extremely difficult to determine precisely what the most serious and demanding instances of human distress are for the minister who seeks to engage himself with hurting persons in helpful ways, for the demands are not always inherently resident in the destructive power of certain situations, but are more dependent upon what types of problems produce a higher degree of anxiety within the individual minister. One minister may become quite anxious and upset over situations that another can handle with genuine confidence and poise, and those that elicit inappropriate and unhelpful responses from the latter may threaten the first not at all.

Nevertheless, almost any minister who has been involved with dying persons and with persons immediately following the death of someone close to them would probably agree that these entail considerable emotional involvement and demand a high degree of sensitivity. The crisis of grief is one in which the minister must participate frequently. There is no escape from it. It is both his burden and his opportunity. It is probably the crisis with which he engages himself most often. If his own feelings in regard to death have not been worked through, he will inevitably find himself handicapped in his ministry. On the one hand, he may allow himself to be pulled into an overinvolvement, an overidentification, in which he feels the pain so intensely himself that it incapacitates him. He becomes anxious, shaky, depressed. On the other hand, to protect himself from the pain, he may insulate himself emotionally to the extent that he is not fully present for the other person. He becomes incapable of genuinely communicating empathy, producing a situation in which all his responses are distorted by his self-protective efforts. The minister must in some way prepare himself emotionally for the experiences of death, dying, and grief. This means, of course, that he must be prepared to look at the reality of his own death in an open manner and accept the full emotional impact of this experience into his own present being.

One beginning checkpoint would be to engage in a detailed fantasy of one's own dying and death, then seek to imagine what it would be like not to be, to picture in one's mind the world simply going on without him. If a person finds himself totally unable to go through such a fantasy in some detail with some degree of reality and emotional response, it may well be that his own feelings about death, his own awareness of himself as a mortal human being, have been too well repressed. An opposite reaction is also possible. In the midst of such fantasy a person begins to find himself overwhelmed by emotion; anxiety rises too strongly; the feelings block the progress of the fantasy or linger on well after the fantasy is concluded or he cannot get his mind off death. In either instance, the minister would be well served as a person and as a professional if he were to talk this over in detail with a competent and sensitive colleague or with some other professional counselor.

THE MINISTER AND THE GRIEF CRISIS

From the point of view of the Christian faith, there are three important motivations for the ministry to the grief-stricken. First, it is the responsibility of the faith to speak to all issues concerning the meaning of life and death, and questions of meaning are raised in a particularly potent way in the experience of grief. Second, the faith itself stimulates the compassion that impels the minister to seek to engage himself with every person in the moment of suffering. Third, an effective ministry to persons at the very time of their grief will save many of these from much distress at a later time.

Unresolved Grief
Related to Physical and Emotional Disorder

A summary of the material elaborating this third point is of significance in establishing the minister's role as the number one, frontline preventive mental health professional in our society and should give him a proper sense of the extreme importance of the work he is doing in his ministry to the bereaved. An increasing mass of research data points to the central motivating force of unresolved grief in a variety of emotional and behavioral disorders.

Physical Illness. A number of studies relate inadequately expressed grief to onset of illnesses characterized by physiological symptoms and physical complaints. In a study of forty-one patients with colitis, Lindemann noted that thirty-three of them had developed the disorder closely following the loss of an emotionally significant person.[1] Parkes, a research psychiatrist at the Tavistock Centre in London, has made extensive studies of the medical records of forty-four widows, comparing the postbereavement period with two years prior to the death of the spouse. The investigation showed a 63 percent increase in the number of visits to the doctor in the first six months after bereavement, and a continued higher rate for the rest of the time studied. This is not at all surprising, however, in the light of the uncomfortable physical symptoms of the grief itself, with a six-month period easily including the peak of the grief reaction. In addition, there was a significant increase in the number of consultations for physical disorders of the arthritic and rheumatoid variety. This in and of itself does not mean an *actual* increase of the pathology, as Parkes recognizes. He does reason, however, that the secondary consequences of grief such as dietary change and the modification of the autonomic functioning may well produce other physiological changes that are the condition for the onset of illness, either in terms of general poor health or in some instances, specific pathology.[2]

Taking a further step beyond the investigation just discussed, Parkes made a study of 4,486 widowers. "Of these, 213 died during the first six months of bereavement, 40% above the expected rate for married men of the same age." This is a confirmation of earlier reports on the higher mortality rate of bereaved persons, and makes the judgment conclusive that the loss of a

---

[1] "Symptomatology and Management of Acute Grief."

[2] C. Murray Parkes, "Effects of Bereavement on Physical and Mental Health—A Study of the Medical Records of Widows," *British Medical Journal*, II (August, 1964), 274-79 (Reprint, 4-5, 6, 13).

mate by death leads to a greater probability of one's own death. Parkes found that the greatest increase in the cause of death was in the group diagnosed as "coronary thrombosis and other arteriosclerotic and degenerative heart disease," with the next highest group diagnosed "other heart and circulatory disease." Of the deaths, 22.5 percent were in the same diagnostic category as the cause of death of the spouses, 23.9 percent higher than the number expected by chance.[3]

Mental Illness. There is also evidence of a causative relationship between the experience of grief which is not fully worked through and the development of mental illness. Moriarty, in his book *Loss of Loved Ones*, states, "It is the thesis of this book that the loss of loved ones, especially through death, is one of the most important causes of major mental illness."[4] Through the data presented in the book, he demonstrates that one of the factors in adult mental illness is the damage to the development of the child by the death of parents or siblings, and that in addition, in the adult, the death of a loved one may actually precipitate an emotional disorder. Detailed data collected and analyzed by Parkes sustain Moriarty's findings. Parkes discovered that the number of mental hospital patients in his investigation whose illness followed the loss of a spouse was six times greater than expected when compared with a nonbereaved population, suggesting bereavement as among causative factors in the illness.[5]

[3] C. Murray Parkes, B. Benjamin, and R. B. Fitzgerald, "Broken Heart: A Statistical Study of Increased Mortality Among Widowers," *British Medical Journal*, I (March, 1969), 740-43 (Reprint, 1, 3-5).

[4] David M. Moriarty, *The Loss of Loved Ones* (Springfield, Illinois: Charles C. Thomas, 1965), p. 13.

[5] C. Murray Parkes, "Recent Bereavement as a Cause of Mental Illness," *British Journal of Psychiatry*, CX (March, 1964), 202.

Family Disorder. Paul, a psychiatrist specializing in family therapy, makes the statement that he has never seen a family in which there was a seriously emotionally disturbed member where there had not been discovered a maladaptive response to object loss by one or more members of the family. Contributing to the emotional disturbance of the mentally ill family member was a pattern of inflexible interaction within the family system, with the presumption being that such forms of interaction were originally responses of denial to the earlier object loss.[6] Assuming the dynamic priority of inadequately expressed grief, Paul developed a treatment modality that sought to bring the grief out into the open where it could be fully experienced by the grief-stricken person and shared by the whole family, with each member of the family brought into the process of empathizing with the grieving family member.[7] This treatment modality for disturbed families has proved to be successful, thus tending to confirm Paul's original thesis that unresolved grief was the root problem, and suggesting an approach to families in grief that might be utilized to advantage by the minister.

Suicide. Several studies of suicide also point to unresolved grief as being a significant motivating factor. One of these reported that 95 percent of the seriously suicidal patients studied had suffered the death or loss under dramatic circumstances of individuals closely related to them. This percentage is contrasted with the control group of patients who were judged not to be

[6] Norman L. Paul and George H. Grosser, "Operational Mourning and Its Role in Conjoint Family Therapy," *Community Mental Health Journal,* I (1965), 340.

[7] Norman L. Paul, "The Use of Empathy in the Resolution of Grief," *Perspectives in Biology and Medicine,* XI (1967), 161.

seriously suicidal and among whom only 40 percent had suffered comparable loss.[8] Another study compared persons who had attempted suicide with those who had actually succeeded in the attempt. The type of loss seemed to make a difference, with twenty-six of the seventy-one attempted suicides having experienced the divorce of their parents and twenty of forty-four of the completed suicides having undergone the death of a parent. When the investigators looked at the increase in seriousness of the suicidal impulses, they found an increasing incidence of loss of a parent by death: suicidal gestures—21 percent, serious attempts —30 percent, completed suicides—45 percent.[9]

The total impact of these findings is that there are a number of areas of possible pathological response that we discover as a result of the unsuccessfully resolved grief crisis. In other words, there is a massive amount of extreme human suffering that takes place over an extended period of time and from which many persons might be saved by timely and effective grief counseling. The minister is the only professional who has the combination of social expectation, professional freedom, and professional training to be of significant help to the greatest percentage of persons in our society in their time of grief. Here, as in a number of other instances, he is the frontline professional: the first (or among the first) to identify and engage himself with persons in distress, working with them in the early stages of crisis, with the possibility of preventing greater breakdown of

[8] Leonard Moss and Donald Hamilton, "The Psychotherapy of the Suicidal Patient," *American Journal of Psychiatry*, CXII (1956), 814-15.

[9] T. L. Dorpat, J. K. Jackson, and H. S. Ripley, "Broken Homes and Attempted and Completed Suicide," *Archives of General Psychiatry*, XII (February, 1965), 213-16.

personal emotional life and interpersonal relations.

The effective meeting of the needs of persons in grief, not only as an immediate humanitarian activity but also as a contribution to the total increase of the mental health of a community and the avoidance of later maladaptive behavior, has begun to be seen by other mental health professionals as an important phase of their work.

In a pilot study one community service took the initiative to contact twenty bereaved families eight days after the death of a family member to offer their counseling services. The stated assumption of the agency was that the persons' usual sources of support would be inadequate at this particular time. The fact that eighteen of the twenty families accepted the offer is probably some kind of judgment upon the ministry of the area. A follow-up questionnaire revealed that twenty-four of the twenty-six family members who responded rated the service as either helpful or very helpful.[10]

We ministers should feel no jealousy over anyone who performs such an obviously helpful service. Nevertheless, we should take this as some criticism of our own failure to perform our traditional and expected functions at the time of death in a conscientious and enlightened manner.

NEEDS OF THE MINISTER
IN WORKING WITH THOSE IN GRIEF

In order to do his work in the alleviation of the pain of grief in the most effective manner, there are several prerequisites for the minister. First, as has already been stated, he must have come to terms with his own feel-

[10] Irwin Gerber, "Bereavement and the Acceptance of Professional Service," *Community Mental Health Journal*, V (1969), 487-95.

ings concerning death and dying, and more precisely *his own* death and dying, and have assimilated these into his own present living. Second, he must have a dedication to persons in pain that compels him to go to suffering persons, using his pastoral initiative courageously, creatively, and sensitively. One aspect of this is the social expectation, the assignment of the social role to the minister as one who should go to people in grief. While placing demands upon him, this role has been given to him as a great gift. The other aspect of the act of going is the minister's own dedication and courage, and only his own personal faith can lead him to that point. Third, he must have an understanding of the dynamics of grief itself, the course of grieving, and the needs of the bereaved persons. Finally, the minister must have some knowledge of the procedures that will enable him to utilize his relationship with the grief sufferer in the most healing way. It is these last two areas which shall comprise the remainder of this chapter.

GRIEF AND THE BEREAVED PERSON

The Dynamics of Grief

A detailed analysis of the dynamics of grief is to be found in an earlier work.[11] In brief summary, the working definition of grief presented there is that it is comparable to a severe attack of anxiety that has as its external stimulus the death of a person with whom one has been closely related. There are three things to note about this proposition. First, grief is like some other experiences that we have. Second, the crucial question to be answered is, "Why does something which happens outside of us cause such a severe painful reaction

[11] Switzer, *The Dynamics of Grief*, pp. 93-177.

within us?" Third, the form in which the relationship is stated implies that there are many emotions involved in our intimate relationships with one another, only one of which is love. Even where there is love, even where love is clearly the predominant emotion, there are always other emotions at work also, and these are either intensified or complicated or both at the time of that person's death. This anxiety of grief is conceived of primarily as a separation anxiety, the prototype experience of which is the first learning on the part of the small infant that the absence of the significant adults in his life inevitably means pain, physical discomfort. The first learning concerning relationships is that the presence of significant other persons means the meeting of personal needs, the sustenance of life, and that the absence of the other is a threat to one's own self. The other person is the major value in any person's life. The loss of the other equals the loss of one's own self. The separation from the person *out there* causes a sense of threat to the self *inside*. Based upon separation anxiety, but usually discussed under another name, is guilt or moral anxiety. There are few, if any, close relationships where each person is always capable of fulfilling all the needs of the other. Therefore, even in the finest relationships, there are at least moments of need frustration, with the attendant feelings of resistance, hostility, or hurt, producing behavior toward each other that is perceived as threatening to the relationship. The experiencing of this threat is the experience of anxiety, but anxiety which in some sense is related to our own behavior, and which is therefore called guilt.

Finally, there is in grief what we term existential anxiety. These are fears arising out of our own existence as human beings, universally shared. They grow out of our

145

freedom, our responsibility for decision, the search for meaning, an awareness of our own finitude, the certainty of our own death. The death of an emotionally significant person serves as a stimulus to bring to the surface this anxiety that is constantly with us but which usually lies well under the surface of our awareness. In the ordinary course of daily life we have devised in our society ways of depersonalizing death and separating ourselves from it. But when someone emotionally close to us dies, these social defenses break down. *This* death has reference to our own lives. In a sense, it is as close as we can come to experiencing our own death while still being able to observe, reflect, and respond to it. This response inevitably contains some fear.

The Needs of the Bereaved

It is self-evident that the complex interplay of the anxiety along with the other emotional reactions in grief produce an intense sense of need in a person who, in fact, at this point is in a state of crisis. It is helpful to the minister to be able to identify the precise needs of the bereaved in order that he may more effectively assist in the process of crisis resolution. Reference has already been made to the role of words in the counseling process. The needs of the bereaved and the procedures of the helping person must be understood in the light of that discussion. Therefore, the major, though not the only method which the pastor uses is to facilitate the verbal expression of the grief sufferer in regard to the deceased, the relationship that existed between them, and the death itself.

The first need is to release negative emotions: hostility, guilt, fear. The need is for catharsis. Speech is a substitute form of the emotionally charged acts that need to be performed, understood, and accepted in the context of relationship with the deceased.

A second need is the affirmation of one's self. Feelings of self-blame and self-depreciation need to be expressed. Lowered feelings of self-esteem need to be raised. Words to another person can be a means of reestablishing one's threatened and disrupted selfhood, since they are the vehicles for reinforcing the attitudes of love and protection toward one's self that were the attitudes of the ones in relationship with whom words were first learned.

The third need is that of breaking the ties with the deceased. This is not as harsh as it may sound at first. It certainly does not mean forgetting the deceased person or not loving that person any longer. Rather, it means a transformation of the act of love. If we continue to try to love in the same way we did when the person was physically present, directing the emotion outward toward him, then we work ourselves into an emotional trap, for in reality there is no person *out there* to receive it in the same sense that there once was. The need is to direct such love for the deceased inward to the images of that person that remain within us, with the outward expression being directed toward others. This last statement introduces the next two needs.

The fourth need is the resurrection of the deceased within the self. To the extent that persons have been emotionally involved with each other, to that degree have they identified their lives with each other. This means that one's own self has certain aspects of the life of the other as a living component. Yet this life of the other within us need not die along with his or her physical body, although this is the first emotional reaction to the death. As we move past this first re-

147

sponse, there can be the revival of the life of the other person within the self, and therefore it becomes whole and fully alive once again. The language that has been the communicating link with the other, in being heard by the speaker himself as he talks of the person and the relationship, carries with it the emotional power of the relationship and reinforces the internalized living presence of the other.

Once this is done, the next need is to direct one's emotions outward in the renewal and deepening of old relationships and occasionally the establishing of new ones. In the midst of the sense of deadness and threat that we feel when someone close to us dies, we need an added portion of this high quality of interpersonal sharing.

Finally, there is a need for the rediscovery of meaning. This is not the introduction of an entirely new element at this point. It is merely using another set of terms to refer to the process of meeting these first five needs. The basic meaning in one's life is essentially emotional and relational. This is precisely what the first five needs refer to. Nevertheless, and this is the second level of meaning, the human being naturally seeks to express his perception of his experiences in some coherent way which makes sense to him and which enables him to express the meaning of his experience to others. It is a human necessity to put our experiences into meaningful symbols which then become reinforcing to the entire process. This is accomplished largely through the use of language.[12]

Understanding these needs of the bereaved as the tasks to be accomplished in grief counseling and an awareness of the relationship of the bereaved person's

[12] *Ibid.*, pp. 195-207.

talking to the fulfilling of these needs set clearly before the minister the specific goals that he should help the grieving person attain and point to an important aspect of his methodology.

The Stages of Grief

Other important guidance is offered to the minister in the methodology of grief counseling by the knowledge of the stages of grief, their characteristics, and the extent in time of the normal grief reaction. The following information is based upon a study which was conducted and reported by Parkes, and grows out of extensive personal interviews with twenty-two widows at the end of the first, third, sixth, ninth, and thirteenth months after their loss by death of their husbands.[13]

The first phase is that of *numbness and denial*. A feeling of numbness was described by ten of the widows and lasted anywhere from one day to more than a month, with five to seven days being the most common. Sixteen of the widows reported difficulty in accepting the fact that their husbands were really dead. Even though numbness is a relatively transient phenomenon, some form of denial of the full reality of what had happened tended to persist. Even after a year, thirteen of the widows said that there were still times when they had difficulty in believing their husbands to be dead.

The second phase is that of *yearning*. In this stage are noted the sense of intense longing and preoccupation with thoughts of the deceased person. The widows often had haunting memories of the final illness or the

[13] C. Murray Parkes, " 'Seeking' and 'Finding' a Lost Object," *Social Science and Medicine*, IV (1970), 187-201.

death. There was the direction of much attention toward places and objects associated with the lost person. Ten of the widows thought that they had heard or seen their husbands during the first month after the death, and sixteen reported a sense of the presence of their husbands near them during the first month. This was still present in twelve widows a year later. Twelve of the widows reported attacks of panic. As might be expected, there were a variety of physiological disturbances during this time, as well as self-reproach, general irritability, or bitterness, a disruption of social relationships, restlessness, and tension. Methods of the mitigation of or defense against loss were varied: partial disbelief in the reality of external events, the inhibition of painful thoughts, selective forgetting, identification as shown in the tendency to behave or think more like their husbands did, dreams of the husband, with happy dreams of interaction with him being far more common than unpleasant ones. This phase begins with the diminishing of the numbness of the first stage and an increase in the intensity of affect and usually lasts for several weeks.

The third phase is that of *disorganization and despair*. This phase is less clearly delineated than the first two because its features are less dramatic. It seems to be introduced as the intensity of yearning and the sharpness of emotion diminish, and some degree of apathy and aimlessness begins to take over. Even one year after bereavement, fifteen of the twenty-two widows declared that they still preferred not to think about the future, and five more regarded their future as distinctly unpleasant. This "no future" orientation seems to characterize the phase.

The final phase is that of the *reorganization of be-*

havior, characterized by a greatly diminished symptomatology, the opening up of the future, a sense that
life has a good taste to it again. However, this does not
come as rapidly as has commonly been thought. A summary of the situation after thirteen months showed loneliness still to be a very common problem. Social adjustment was rated by the interviewer as good in five instances, fair in nine, poor in eight. Six widows had
definitely worse health than before the death of their
husbands, and none was healthier. Six reported themselves being happy, seven as sad, two as neutral, and
seven as having moods that fluctuated between happi-
ness and sadness. In terms of overall adjustment, the
interviewer made the judgment that three were very
poorly adjusted, depressed, and grieving a great deal,
nine were intermittently disturbed and depressed, six
showed a tenuous adjustment which might be easily
upset, and four had made a good adjustment. The
conclusion is that even after thirteen months the process of grieving was still going on, and although the
principle features were all past their peak, there was
no sense in which grief could be said to have finished.

One of the important observations that was made as
a result of the study had to do with differences in the
degree of the overt expression of emotional distress immediately following the loss and the longer-term outcome with regard to emotional adjustment. The group
of widows with the mildest forms of emotional expression during the first week of bereavement grew to be the
most disturbed in the third month. During the period
of six to nine months it was impossible to distinguish
them from the two groups who were moderately and
severely disturbed initially.

However, toward the end of the year the first group

again became more disturbed, and after the end of the year, three out of the five widows in this group were now moderately or severely disturbed. In contrast, only one of the eight widows who were in the initial moderate affect group and three of the nine in the initial severe affect group were similarly disturbed. *It is difficult to avoid the conclusion that early full griev-ing, the overt exhibiting of emotional behavior, pro-duces a reduction in later symptoms of disturbance, while the repression or covering up of initial affect leads to a greater severity of those feelings when they finally do emerge.*

Practical Implications for the Minister

Parkes' findings make several contributions to the minister concerned with the practical aspects of grief counseling. First, they confirm that rather severe emo-tional disturbance and behavioral problems, which un-der other circumstances we might judge as being severe to an abnormal degree, are actually normal in the grief reaction. For the minister to know this will, first, reduce his own anxiety in the pastoral relationship with the grieving person whose emotions are being quite strongly expressed or whose behavior seems unusual, and sec-ond, enable him to help the grieving person accept his or her own feelings or behavior, since one of the initial fears of many grieving persons is that they are abnormal or are losing their minds.

Second, the findings of this study confirm that the earlier full grieving takes place the more likely it is that there will be a significant reduction in later symptoms of disturbance. This not only gives the minister permis-sion but actually encourages him to seek from the very beginning to facilitate in an active manner the emotional expressions of bereaved persons.

Third, the findings demonstrate very clearly that even after thirteen months the process of grieving was still going on, and although the principle features were all past their peak, there was no sense in which grief could be said to be concluded. Overall, the evidence seems to support the hypothesis that early and regular pastoral care and counseling would in fact, other factors being equal, enable a person to move through the stages of grief more rapidly and with less severe persisting symptoms of disturbance.

An additional study points up even other factors to be aware of in the process of grief work when the loss takes place in any way within a family setting, as is usually the case.

The importance of the death of a person for his family has been recognized and has become the basis of a research project in which crisis intervention teams of mental health professionals would visit families no later than twelve hours after the death of the member, then seek to see them as a whole family for two to six sessions over a period of one to ten weeks. "This short-term intervention is aimed at increasing the effectiveness of the family in coping with feelings, decisions, and subsequent adjustment related to the death." [14] For research purposes nonintervention crisis and noncrisis control groups have been selected. While results are not yet conclusive, since at this writing the study has not been completed, initial data show trends that support the initial emphasis on the importance of the fam-

[14] Rita R. Vollman, Amy Ganzert, Lewis Picher, and W. Vail Williams, "The Reactions of Family Systems to Sudden and Unexpected Death," *Omega*, II (May, 1971), 101.

ily as a single whole system, an organism in and of itself, and upon the successful reassignment of roles within the system as being of major significance in the health of the family and its individual members.[15] This task of assisting the family in the redistribution of roles becomes a self-conscious focus of intervention in grief. It should not be overlooked that children are very much a part of the family, and while their roles are not usually as instrumental and task-oriented as those of adults, the social-emotional roles they have are of crucial influence in the life of the family.[16] The whole family, including the children, must be led in grief counseling to a realignment of roles as a necessary adjustment to loss.

The functions of the minister in the grief situation then are to be based on the data presented up to this point:

1. the need for the immediate initiation of the facilitation of the grieving process;
2. the overall long-term needs of the bereaved and an understanding, not only of how the person's crying and other nonverbal emotional expressions may be elicited, but also of how extensive talking within the pastoral relationship enables those needs to be met more quickly and more fully;
3. the concept of crisis that has been derived originally from a study of grief, and the effectiveness of crisis intervention as an active, frequently directive, form of counseling in contrast with a more passive, nondirective modality;
4. the extent of time in the course of normal grieving;

[15] *Ibid.*, pp. 104-5. Also W. Vail Williams, Paul Polak, and Rita R. Vollman, "Crisis Intervention in Acute Grief," *Omega*, III (February, 1972), 69-70.
[16] Vollman, et. al., "The Reactions of Family Systems," 104.

5. the needs of the child who has lost someone significant in his life and the importance of attention to his grieving;
6. the values of a family interaction approach to grief which takes place in a family matrix, the effectiveness in the healing of grief of shared empathy within the family, and the need to work consciously at the reassignment of roles within the family.

THE PRACTICAL FUNCTIONING OF THE MINISTER

The Schedule of Pastoral Care

A schedule of grief counseling could look something like the following, recognizing some considerable variation because of different external circumstances and differences in individual needs and responses. The minister should contact the family or grief-stricken person just as soon as he hears of the death, and it would be well to make a personal visit. What takes place in this call will vary considerably. It may under some circumstances be quite brief with nothing of observable significance occurring. The significant thing is that, on a personal level and also as the representative of the Christian community, the minister has been there and has come as quickly as possible, communicating to the bereaved the priority of the event in the mind of the minister and the life of the community. If in this visit there has been no reasonable period of time for conversation or no substantial amount of overt expression of emotion or no opportunity to talk about the death, the dead person, the relationship, the funeral, then there must be a second prefuneral call, scheduled so that sufficient time may be given to these tasks.

Therefore, at the second call prior to the funeral the minister should inquire about and encourage the bereaved person or persons to talk about the death and its circumstances. The minister should be prepared to receive anything the bereaved want to say about the dead person and the relationship. Finally, at some point there must be a focus on the funeral. This discussion must deal with a number of details which at first glance may seem to be irrelevant to the grieving process, and may even be experienced by some ministers as a jarring note and a distasteful duty. However, not only is this necessary for the mechanical details themselves, but there are important opportunities that arise out of such a discussion. First, talking about the funeral in any concrete and detailed way may be an important reinforcement of the reality of the finality of the death that has occurred. Second, by the way in which the minister introduces the discussion, he may directly facilitate talking about the dead person. For example, questions may be asked concerning the form and elements of the service from the point of view of who the dead person was. Did he or she have any specific instructions concerning the service? Did you ever hear the person express his or her views concerning death or funerals? Did he or she have any favorite passages of scripture or hymns or other music? What sorts of things do you (the grieving person or persons) feel are important about the dead person that I (the minister) should consider in the preparation of the funeral and of a short funeral sermon? Third, the discussion of the funeral with the family provides the context for a declaration of a sustaining and hope-stimulating faith as the funeral is interpreted and developed along with them as a service of worship to God and not just a religiously oriented memorial ceremony.

A third step in the schedule of grief counseling is the funeral itself. Putting it in this way indicates clearly that the funeral should not be conceived of by the minister apart from pastoral relationships nor should counseling in some formal way be separated from the funeral. The funeral becomes an outmoded, meaningless, distasteful custom *only* if ministers and congregations allow it to become that. It may be, indeed *must* be, and *can* be, a vital element in the grieving process. The guidelines contained in Irion's superb book for evaluating a funeral contain ten highly significant criteria arranged under social, psychological, and theological needs to be met.[17] These all relate to the effective healing of grief and the maintenance of community. Every minister should have these before him as he prepares for a funeral.

The fourth step which the minister should take in order to facilitate the grieving process is a postfuneral call within two or three days following the service. This is frequently the first occasion offering sufficient time for an extended conversation in some reasonably quiet setting without many interruptions. It will often reflect back on the funeral and the bereaved's responses to it, and this may be the springboard into more detailed talking about the dead person and the relationship and more overt expression of emotion.

Finally, there should be continued regular pastoral conversations, approximately weekly during the first six weeks and then moving to perhaps every ten days to

[17] Paul E. Irion, *The Funeral: Vestige or Value* (Nashville: Abingdon Press, 1966), pp. 117-19.

two weeks for another six weeks or so, and then tapering off into less frequent contacts as grief work seems to be in the process of being accomplished, the pain diminishing somewhat, and activities and relationships being renewed. If there seems to be absolutely no, or relatively little, diminishing of the grief behavior after about three months, then serious consideration should be given to bringing a professional counselor into the picture.

While on the basis of the data clarifying the needs of the bereaved, no pastor would disagree that a schedule something like this should be followed, the issue of time raises its perennial ugly head. If you are the only pastor in a church where there are several deaths each month, or on the staff of a large church which includes an aging membership, and especially in a city where there are many funerals of persons who are not members of your congregation, how can such a schedule possibly be followed? One, or a combination of three, ways should be considered. 1) Where there is a church staff, responsibility for grief counseling might be relatively evenly shared by all staff members, or one staff member with particular sensitivities and skills might be relieved of some other responsibilities in order to pursue this one most effectively. 2) Lay persons may also be trained in grief counseling and assigned to visit persons or families regularly throughout the mourning period. 3) The minister may bring those grieving persons who are willing into a grief work group, not only saving some of his own time, but in fact rendering a different and in some ways a higher quality of service to those in distress.

The Methodology of Pastoral Care

The final section of this chapter will seek to deal in an even more concrete manner with the specific methodology of the minister's grief counseling, his actual functioning with the bereaved. First, recognizing the particular nature of the event of death, it should be declared that the broad methodological base out of which the minister's grief counseling activities arise is the outgrowth of client-centered therapy and of crisis intervention. The work of Carkhuff has been referred to earlier in the context of his offering the several essential ingredients for all effective helping relationships. Of these, those most relevant for the early stages of grief counseling are accurate empathy, respect, genuineness, and concreteness. Most people in grief will initially be sufficiently expressive of affect, so the pastor's responses that reflect accurate empathy and respect will cement the relationship for further dimensions of counseling and assist continued and deeper affective expressions. The minister should, of course, be prepared to receive great amounts of painful emotion. The primary methodology then, especially in these early stages of counseling, although certainly not the exclusive one, is the attempt to reflect back to the person in an accurate way the verbal meaning and the specific affect and the degree of intensity of affect of his communications. This type of response is facilitative of further and fuller affective expression and of increased depth of self-exploration. If there is not such free flow of emotion on the part of the bereaved person, the minister should move on into the more directive procedures of crisis intervention.

At this point, there is more verbal activity on the part of the counselor, more initiative, questioning, active searching for behavioral alternatives, decision-making. In line with this, in grief work there should be from the very beginning a focus on the memories, images, and emotions surrounding the death of the person: the illness, the accident; the way the person looked and sounded; what took place, what was said; the death itself. The bereaved person should be encouraged by any means to talk about as much of this as possible. He should be helped to review his own emotional and behavioral reactions at that time. Direct and forceful questioning will usually not be needed. Grieving persons often offer just such material as this. If they do not, however, they will ordinarily respond to soft and gentle suggestions, particularly elicited by the minister's warm and sincere interest and concern about what has taken place. In those relatively few instances where the bereaved persons are only minimally responsive, understanding that at this point we are talking about pastoral counseling sessions that follow the first postfuneral call, more direct and forceful questions and suggestions that lead into the review of memories, images, and emotions surrounding the death should be used. This should certainly not be interpreted to mean insensitivity to a person's proper privacy or harshness or hard confrontation, but it is the combination of genuine interest, an openness to receive even negative and strong emotion, and whatever persistent directiveness may be necessary.

As minister and bereaved move past the events surrounding the death and the funeral, they should enter into a phase of reviewing the relationship between the bereaved and the dead person. The grief sufferer should be assisted in recounting everything he or she possibly can concerning the relationship. The minister will need to persist in asking for concreteness, for specific examples, for details of remembered events, scenes, and encounters. A full elaboration should be encouraged. And all the way through he should attend to affect and facilitate its full expression. The minister must be very careful that he does not allow his own feelings of anxiety and uneasiness in the presence of painful experiences and emotions to produce behavior on his part which will reinforce the telling about only the good aspects of the relationship, forcing the person to squelch the negative feelings, the conflicts, the unpleasant and unfulfilling aspects, with the effect of stimulating even more guilt about having such feelings. The minister should always be prepared to be patient with repetition. Frequently the repetition of events or certain aspects of the relationship will be necessary in order for negative feelings to come out fully and for the ties to be broken. All these procedures will be elaborated and illustrated in the next chapter.

Finally, when the bereaved person has reached the point of readiness, his movements in the direction of acts of giving up the physical presence of the deceased (the giving away clothes or books or other possessions, the changing of a room) should be affirmed and assisted. So also should any movements toward reentry into old groups and activities and occasionally the taking up of new ones, the reestablishing and deepening of friendships and occasionally the establishment of new relationships.

As suggested earlier, special attention should be given to the children in a family where there has been a loss, both when they are with the rest of the family and when they are alone. In addition, work with the entire family should be emphasized, using as much as possible something of the schedule and procedures already described, but recognizing that there will be numerous practical barriers standing in the way of any ideal accomplishment of this goal. One procedure growing out of the work of Paul suggests that we encourage the family members one by one to share their grief fully with one another. As each one does so, the others are assisted in expressing their empathy with that person. After feelings are fully expressed, the realignment of family roles will need to be raised, and the family members assisted in the decision-making necessary to accomplish this. While some families handle this very important group task rather effectively, some may fall into a trap. Some may tend unconsciously to enter into collusion in seeking to assign the total need-fulfilling role of the deceased to one individual member rather than allotting the functions more appropriately to those persons most capable of meeting the particular needs. Others may contain an individual who unconsciously identifies with the deceased to such a degree that he seeks to assume the total role.[18] For some families, a simple open discussion of their need to relate to one another in somewhat different ways now that one of them has died will be sufficient to head off this potential problem. For some it will be more complex, and it may be that some professional other than the minister will need to be consulted. But the conscientious minister has a crucial function to play as he perceives the new family interaction and guides them toward the help they need.

An especially important aspect of the minister's grief counseling is his utilization of his understanding of the inter- and intrapersonal dynamics of leave-taking. This involves the strategy for breaking away from his intensive relationship with the bereaved with whom he has been working during the period of grief and its resolution. The self-conscious use of the termination of the

[18] George Krupp, "Maladaptive Reactions to the Death of a Family Member," *Social Casework*, LIII (July, 1972), 433.

counseling relationship with its dimensions of interpersonal depth is an important contribution to the mourning process itself and one which most ministers probably have overlooked, although undoubtedly many sensitive pastors have in fact functioned in very helpful ways at this end stage of grief counseling without always being fully aware of the double significance of what was taking place.

The understanding of the relation of bereavement itself and the termination of counseling has been developed in a very lucid and helpful way by Loewald in psychoanalytic terms. In any leave-taking or separation, he states that

an attempt is made to deny loss: either we try to deny that the other person still exists or did exist, or we try to deny that we have to leave the beloved person and venture out on our own. . . . In true mourning, the loss of the beloved person is perhaps temporarily denied but gradually is accepted and worked out by way of a complex inner process.[19]

This has already been discussed to some extent in relationship to loss by death. What takes places in counseling of any depth is that a relationship of significance and intense emotion is established, and when the counseling ceases, the relationship either comes to an end or at least changes radically. Leave-taking must be accomplished. There is a loss of a significant other person. As pastor and counselee move into the last few sessions, such loss begins to be anticipated, and anxious feelings similar to those of grief (in this case, anticipatory grief) begin to be experienced. "The extended leave-taking at the end phase of analysis is a replica of the process of

---

[19] Hans W. Loewald, "Internalization, Separation, Mourning, and the Superego," *Psychoanalytic Quarterly*, XXXI (1962), 485.

mourning." [20] This last statement is the key to understanding how an effective termination of counseling assists the process of mourning itself for which the counseling was taking place.

It is absolutely essential that the parting be made explicit in words, that the emotions be expressed, the meaning of the relationship be articulated, and that good-bye be said in a clear and appropriate way. When this is done, "then neither the existence of the person from whom we part nor the anticipated life without him can be denied." [21] Due to the quality of relationship that a pastor establishes with a bereaved person, especially if he carries through with the full course of grief work as suggested in this chapter, it is not uncommon for the counselor to be placed unconsciously by the bereaved in some aspect of the role of the dead person. To the extent that the pastoral counselor recognizes this behavior, it provides the opportunity to help the bereaved person understand that he is seeking to deny the death by externalizing aspects of the dead person that are actually living parts of the bereaved's own self. In other words, the reaction of denial, which to some degree is a part of every grief, like all repression, is never fully effective. That which is directly denied begins to express itself in some way in overt behavior. In the grief counseling relationship the repressed elements of the lost person begin to be externalized, expressed in some form of the contemporary transactions taking place between the pastor and the grief sufferer. These are recognized by the counselor, discussed with the person in terms of their meaning in this present relationship, and thus it becomes possi-

[20] *Ibid.*, 485-86.
[21] *Ibid.*, p. 485.

ble for the bereaved person to accept them as a part of himself in a new form. Denied aspects of the deceased's life are gotten out, recognized for what they are, then taken back into one's self. "It seems that emancipation as a process of separation from external objects . . . goes hand in hand with the work of internalization which reduces or abolishes the sense of external deprivation and loss."[22] Effective mourning involves not only certain aspects of *relinquishing* the lost person, but also of allowing those aspects of the other person which through identification have become a part of the very selfhood of the bereaved to become fully alive, and of receiving the lost person in a new way. When this begins to happen, grief work is moving toward its conclusion. Yet the end of counseling is something of a replica of this process, and can be consciously utilized by the pastoral counselor as a repetition of the loss by death. A conscious leave-taking between the pastor and the bereaved can begin to take place in the form of an explicit discussion of how they feel about the cessation of the counseling relationship itself. As this is done, the original grief for which the counseling has been taking place may be more adequately healed.

Now this sounds rather complex, but all it refers to is the fact that certain unconscious elements of one's own self in relationship to the deceased have now become conscious in relationship with the pastoral counselor. By experiencing them consciously, expressing one's feelings concerning them, and recognizing them for what they are, they become transformed into living sources of meaning and strength which may be consciously incorporated by the person into his present behavior and relationships.

[22] *Ibid.*, p. 490.

It would seem that the minister's strategy with the grief-stricken might be to make the somewhat frequent visits to which reference has already been made, beginning in the midst of the crisis itself, when a person is both highly vulnerable and in need of support, as well as open to influence by another caring person. Because of the heightened emotions of the grief crisis, a relationship of meaning and depth is rapidly established. In this relationship elements of the bereaved's relations with other significant persons, often including the deceased, are introduced, making this material available for further discussion, with a dual focus on the relationship with the deceased and the present relationship with the pastor. As the number and frequency of the visits decrease, the minister refers to this and to the eventual ending of this form of their relationship. This makes possible a reliving of a leave-taking, with the minister's being attentive to all the important aspects of such a separation, encouraging a full expression of all the feelings involved, including his own. Such a process enables the mourner to assimilate in something of the same way and as a part of his own being, aspects of this present relationship with the pastor as well as to complete the mourning process initiated by the death of an emotionally significant person. The minister, of course, realizes that more often than not, when he is counseling with a bereaved person, they are moving toward a transformation of the relationship rather than the total termination of it. Nevertheless, when it has been as intense and meaningful as it has been in grief counseling, even such transformation entails the anticipation of object loss from the perspective of the counselee.

When the minister engages in grief counseling, he

must always be aware of the fact that he does so in the context of a faith-stance toward life which has a dynamic meaning to it. The psalmist says, "As for man, his days are like grass; he flourishes like a flower of the field; for the wind passes over it, and it is gone, and its place knows it no more" (103:15-16). This is certainly the description of each one of us. We are here and then we are gone. And gone also in a physical sense are those whom we love and with whom we have had conflict and with whom we have shared many aspects of our lives. Yet this is not the whole of the psalmist's message. These words are set in the midst of an affirmation of faith in the Lord who "knows our frame; he remembers that we are dust." Then he goes on to proclaim, "The steadfast love of the Lord is from everlasting to everlasting upon those who fear him" (103: 14, 17). The nature of human existence seems to be that a person is never left totally without possibilities. There may be other ways of saying it, in fact there *are*, but a person of faith can declare with the psalmist that the continual existence of possibilities is reflection of faith in God as active love and man's possibilities in any situation as being God's gift. The anxiety of grief not only has potential destructive powers, but like any anxiety, may have a primary function to produce growth in human life, including growth in faith. It can be the painful stimulus that leads a person to resources that not only can heal but make new. It is given to the ministers of God the opportunity to be servants in this process of healing and renewal in the central crisis of human existence, that of death and grief.

Chapter VI

INTERVENTION IN A PATHOLOGICAL GRIEF CRISIS REACTION

(A Case Study)

This chapter is an attempt to illustrate how a counseling strategy might be developed and applied by a minister in a specific situation of grief.[1] The case material presented here has both the advantages and disadvantages of an extreme reaction. It demonstrates that even in quite difficult instances progress in the alleviation of maladaptive behavior may be achieved, even though in a number of respects the case is not typical of that with which the minister usually deals. Nevertheless, once given a particular situation, in the light of the needs of all bereaved persons and the suggested possible methodologies of intervention, the minister must make a series of decisions as to the most intense needs, those that may be met most readily, and his own means of relating helpfully to that person or family and the persons within the family. The following case study illustrates how some of these decisions are made and what

[1] This chapter is based on the author's article, "Repressed Affect and Memory Reactive to Grief: A Case Fragment," originally published in *Omega:* An International Journal for Study of Death and Lethal Behavior, III (Spring, 1972), 121-26.

the procedures look like in action. We would do well to keep in mind, too, that although the pastoral counselor involved in this case came into the situation of morbid grief reaction several months after the funeral, parish ministers themselves do in fact have to deal with extreme behavior in response to bereavement, and often they have not been involved with the persons in a pastoral relationship prior to the time that they are called into the situation.

The operation of the mechanisms of denial and the repression of affect and even of memory surrounding the death of a person with whom one has been closely tied emotionally has been observed by almost every person who is frequently involved with the bereaved. Therefore, it should be clear that the purpose of this report of the losses of a twenty-year-old female psychiatric patient is not to go through the superfluous activity of seeking to demonstrate that such repression *can* happen, but, first, to portray a rather unique combination of such repressions, having the effect of producing an almost total amnesia for the details of a relationship that had existed since the patient's birth. Second, however, another purpose is even more important to the parish minister. That is to introduce in the context of this case a methodology for the facilitation of grief work which can be utilized not only in severe cases such as this, but which is adaptable to the counseling procedures in dealing with "normal" grief, beginning at the time of the loss, and in the hope of preventing "morbid" grief reactions.

This young woman was admitted to a psychiatric hospital on the basis of about five months of moderate depression reactive to a series of events: anticipatory grief during the several-month terminal illness of her grandfather, with whom she had had an unusually close emotional relationship, the breaking off of a romance by her boyfriend, and the death of her grandfather about a month later.

The patient was the first child of her parents. A congenital disorder required rather constant attention which continued because of parental anxiety even after the disorder was corrected. This attention was drastically and suddenly curtailed by the birth of the next sibling when the patient was about three, and then further diminished by a third child. One can presume the sense of deprivation that this small child must have felt as the exclusive and intense care that had been given to her was now shared with others.

When she was fifteen, she left her own home to live with her maternal grandparents in the same city, the reason given being the availability in another high school with a better department in the field of her major interest. In this home she was once again the exclusive center of attention, reproducing the situation of the first three years of her life. The grandfather became the focal point of her affection.

The contemporary events of loss began, when in the patient's second year of college, the grandfather was hospitalized with cancer. Although the patient knew of this, she was not informed of its critical nature until several weeks after his admission, when she was actually in the car going to visit him for the first time. This tardy statement did not prepare her at all for the shock of seeing his debilitated body and his inability even to recognize her. She remained in the room only briefly, recoiling in horror. She never returned to see him.

Within several weeks the young man with whom she was in love simply stopped seeing her and calling her.

When the impact of this broken relationship hit her, she made a mild suicide attempt, rather obviously communicative-manipulative in nature, reflective of her genuine feelings of abandonment and despair, but she reported later that there was the equally genuine feeling of not wanting to kill herself *dead*.

Within another few weeks the grandfather died. The precise beginning point of her depression could not be identified. It had apparently been in the process of development during his hospitalization and prior to the breaking of her relationship with the young man and had never lifted, although she was never totally nonfunctional in it. After about three more months, during which she saw a psychiatrist several times, she was admitted to the hospital.

It was judged that although there was an underlying, long-term, and deep emotional need that would call for continued treatment, a noticeable raising of mood and mobilization of ego resources might be accomplished by means of intensive crisis therapy focusing on her recent experiences of loss, since, with the exception of the acting out of the suicide attempt, they had never been openly expressed, certainly not in a direct manner. It was hypothesized that the loss of the grandfather was primary, first, chronologically, because it in fact dated from her experience in the hospital room, and second, because of the lifelong relationship. It was not implausible to consider the hypothesis that her anticipatory grief reactions were of such a nature as to have played some role in the withdrawal of the boyfriend, although no data were obtained to substantiate such a presupposition.

A minister was available to talk with her in the hospital. His decision was to see her twice a week, forty-five minutes to an hour, for three weeks, with an exclusive focus being on her grief reaction to the loss of her grandfather, then, if progress were made, to move to the loss of the boyfriend and the suicide gesture. The therapeutic relationship and the methodology employed were planned in accordance with the needs of bereaved persons, as previously discussed, and the rationale for stimulating the grief sufferer to talk as soon as possible and as fully as possible about the dead person, the relationship, and the death events. With this patient a clear contract was made concerning the focus of the talks and the number of sessions. Such a contract would not usually be made in the "normal" or the nonpathological grief reaction, when one presumes that a person's grief work will be done with several others, of whom the minister is only one, in several structured and nonstructured social settings, and over a period of several months.

A very strong distrust of and anger at the hospital on the part of the patient was evident at the beginning and continued throughout the interviews. However, the minister was not officially related to the hospital, and the young woman was genuinely responsive to the attempt of someone to talk with her about her grandfather, something that she had avoided, but felt was important. One must not overlook, however, her hidden agenda which became apparent a bit later, her search for an ally to help her in her struggle against the hospital staff and in her attempt to be discharged.

The first task was to seek to elicit the affect that one would normally expect during the time of anticipatory grief and the initial grief reaction itself through the exploration of the illness, the death, and the immediate postdeath experiences, including the funeral. This beginning point is based upon the rather well-established evidence that the shock and denial, which is the usual first reaction to the death of an emotionally related person, is the attempt to deal with the intense anxiety of loss and its threat to the self. In most instances, shock and denial are not capable of handling the combined power of the internal feelings and the external reality of the death. The next normal phase of grief, then, is an outpouring of emotion, the feeling and the expression of pain, the variety of emotions not always clearly differentiated and identified at this point, but yet a rather uninhibited cathartic expression which is initially tension-relieving and door-opening to more specific exploration. When this has not taken place, as it had not with this patient, further stages of grief work cannot be accomplished. Therefore, the methodology of the counselor is to ask the grief sufferer to recount as much detail as possible about the death and the events surrounding it, pressing always for more detail and for the expression of the feelings that the person might have been experiencing at the time. This is a very directive, sensitively aggressive lancing of a psychic wound that is still festering. To use terms like directive and aggressive is not at all in conflict with the central role of the accurate communication of empathy which is seen by Carkhuff and others as the absolutely essential ingredient of all effective helping relationships, as has been discussed earlier.

Following this cathartic expression, and including inevitably the beginning of self-exploration concerning the relationship between the grieved person and the deceased, one's feelings about one's self and the other, a complete review of the relationship is the next appropriate phase. Again, the procedure is to take an active role in asking the bereaved person about the deceased, about him as a person, about their relationship, asking again in detail for all the possibly significant memories, what they did together, what they said, what the bereaved person felt at the time, the meaning of all this for her.

With the young woman suffering from depression, an unexpected barrier was discovered almost from the very beginning. Not only could she not presently respond with the appropriate affect, not only had she repressed the actual feelings, but she had repressed even the memory of having had feelings at all. Indeed, she had little memory of most of the events surrounding her grandfather's death, and had lost *almost all memory of the events of her lifelong relationship with him.* The selective nature of this memory loss must be emphasized, because memory loss in general was not a part of her clinical picture. It was only in regard to her grandfather.

She did recall the shock of seeing in the hospital what she reported as the wasted body of what had been her grandfather ("It was not really him." Denial.), his inability even to recognize her, and her leaving the room to vent her anger at her family for not having prepared her for this and for their present open discussion of his impending death (her response to what was seen as a challenge to her denial). She could remember her father's telling her of the grandfather's death, but could not feel presently or recall her feelings at the time. She had gone to the funeral home alone, refusing to go with any of the family, reporting that she would not put herself in the position of being with anyone else when she was feeling deeply and might have to express her emotions in their presence: "It's a sign of weakness." When

174

questioned persistently about what she experienced when she stood alone before his body, it was interesting to note that she responded fairly readily that her only memory of affect was that of anger: "I was mad at him because he had left my grandmother alone." It was only in a later session that she was able to say that she was angry at him for leaving *her*. As far as the funeral was concerned, the patient remembered attending, but details of the event and her feelings before, during, and after were not available to her.

This type of directive attempt to stimulate her self-exploration was carried out through persistent and specific questioning, reflective responses attentive to affect, and statements which were intended to be invitational to affect. ("I think if I were in such a situation I would feel . . ." "That would make me feel . . .") This type of statement would tend to have the effect of giving permission to feel and express loss, guilt, sadness, anger. Three aspects of the patient's behavior during this first session need to be noted. First, she was not without feeling, apathetic. Several times feelings would begin to rise to the surface in the direction of expression and would be cut off. To the extent that these were attempts to *remember* and *relive* feelings at the time of the grandfather's illness and death, the mechanism seemed to be that of repression. When the affect was genuinely contemporary, at the moment she talked, there was much more conscious suppression, prior conditioning to fight one's own feelings and not to let them out for others, or even one's own self, to see and experience fully. Second, she herself seemed genuinely astonished and baffled by her inability to remember what had gone on and how she had felt, as if she had even put out of her mind up until this point the idea that she even *should* try to remember. Third, positive transference toward the minister began to develop quite rapidly.

In the second session, the minister made the decision to move on to the second phase of grief counseling, that of reviewing the whole relationship between the grief sufferer and the dead person, even though obviously phase one was incomplete. It was judged that further direct confrontation with the events of the death would meet with continued unconscious resistance, and, since time was limited, that the approach to the painful emotions might be made by withdrawing to earlier, more pleasant memories. Then the counselor could lead the patient chronologically back to the illness and death, with the ego now being strengthened by some reinforcement of earlier "good objects," earlier relationships and experiences and responses of significant other persons that one has taken into himself as a part of his own self image. Also during this second phase, the relationship between the patient and the minister could continue to develop and perhaps aid in facilitating the exploration of the repressed painful affect. The grandfather had been spoken of in quite idealistic terms. According to the patient, the relationship with him had been a most meaningful one all her life. When she was a child they had done many things. He was always there. He was available, but *he did not bother her or make demands of her*. Following the principle of concreteness as a necessary facilitative condition for effective psychotherapy, the patient was asked to describe specifically and in detail events in her relationship with her grandfather. What did they do together? What did they talk about? Recount times together, activities, conversations. The first response, with some amazement to herself, was, "I don't know. I can't. I can't remember." After persistent pushing by the minister for memories and images, only four could be reproduced. One, when the patient was small, he occasionally took her to the carnival. Two, he took her fishing a few times, but in fact, she did not like to go fishing. Three, she could remember him in his chair watching television. Four, she talked with him about her problems, but pressing for detail revealed that it was actually her grand*mother* who talked with her. No more information was forthcoming concerning what had taken place between them, except that she was quite clear that at no time, even when she was small, did they express their affection for one another in any physical way. Time and again throughout the interview, the patient's reply was, "I don't remember. I just can't."

This degree of memory repression is considerably more than ordinary, extending beyond just the affect and painful events of the death itself to the patient's entire lifetime of relationship with her grandfather, but which, except for a few small fragments, she was unable to document in concrete terms. One might begin to speculate that in addition to the rather obvious repression operating, much of the relationship between the two was one of fantasy and idealization on the part of the patient, not new fantasy and idealization as a part of the grief reaction, which, of course, does happen, but extending from her childhood days, as she sought available love (i.e., need-fulfilling) objects in response to perceived rejection by her parents. A picture of the grandfather began to emerge, as much as the minister could piece together the reality of it, of a man who was rather passive and undemonstrative, who placed no demands on his granddaughter, who could then be viewed in contrast with the parents and idealized. In addition, her own emotional life seemed to be patterned very much after his, the suppression of affect, not allowing the "weakness" of feeling and its expression: identification with partial aspects of the real man as well as the idealized man.

The patient's rather rapid positive transference seemed to be in terms of her feelings toward her grandfather, assisted by the actual role of the minister as not related administratively to the hospital, the negative transference already having been directed at the hospital as personified by her administrative psychiatrist. This double transference was rather strongly demonstrated when she sought to maneuver the minister into the position of taking her side against the hospital, saving her by aiding in her discharge, an apparent reenactment of the utilization of grandparent against parent. The maneuvering ended when the minister proposed this interpretation of the behavior he was observing, and pointed out that the reality of the present situation was such that he could not fulfill this role and that this would not fit their original contract. The full import of the interpretation did not gain immediate full acceptance, but both the comparison of the relationships and the present reality were understood, and it was possible to move on with the grief work.

It became apparent because of the rapid development of the relationship between the patient and the minister that he had the opportunity to use the potency of the relationship and the necessity of a clearcut termination to seek to produce for the patient a model of what separation or objective loss might mean in a healthy form. Referring back to Loewald's comparison of the psychodynamics of mourning and termination of therapy as presented in the last chapter, it was felt that one way of breaking through the patient's strong denial of so much of the relationship with her grandfather and the accompanying repression of affect would be to move with her through an emotionally intense but verbally explicit separation.

At this point in the fourth session, there was the beginning of a breakthrough in the expression of feeling when the minister clearly reminded the patient that they would have only two more sessions, then he, too, would leave her, a repetition of loss. This focus on what was happening at the present moment is the introduction of immediacy as defined by Carkhuff.[2] It produced a series of affective responses, beginning with tears and the statement, "Everyone I really care about leaves me." She was able to say that she was hurting over the anticipated separation from the counselor. In this context, she began to discuss how difficult it was for her to say good-bye. This was followed by the first realization that she had not told her grandfather good-bye, knowing now that she could have visited him earlier in the hospital, that she did not because of her own need to deny what was taking place, accepting her responsibility, and beginning to feel her guilt about it. Once again she reflected upon seeing his body at the funeral home and feeling anger "because he had left *me* alone," the *me* replacing the *grandmother* of her earlier statement. It was suggested that she might well have feelings of anger at the minister at the present time because he was leaving her, but she reported not experiencing this.

The fifth session picked up on the separation theme

[2] *Helping and Human Relations*, Vol. 1, pp. 173-75; Vol. II, pp. 94-95.

and how people separate from one another. An attempt was made by the counselor to enable her to say good-bye to her grandfather *now*, both by asking the question, "What would you like to tell him now?" ("I don't know") and then asking her to see the minister as the grandfather and talk directly to him ("I can't do it"). Finally, the minister asked, "How are you going to say good-bye to me?" Again, "I don't know," but her deep expression of hurt and her tears began to show that she was opening up to the possibility of *feeling* her emotions and expressing them openly and directly. The next procedural steps in the last session would be to attempt to link this present relationship, the separation, and the experiencing and expression of this loss and its good-bye—including its hurt, threat, and anger—to what went on at the loss of her grandfather and her boyfriend.

However, before the final session her parents came to the hospital, requested her discharge, and took her home. She and the minister never said good-bye. Nevertheless, the progress made during the sessions points to the efficacy of the methodology used by the minister, combining in short-term crisis counseling the essential ingredients that Carkhuff has pointed to as necessary for any helping process, the directive and active aspects of crisis intervention in general as applied to the specific needs of the bereaved person as stated earlier, and finally drawing upon the explicit termination of the counseling relationship as a means of enabling a person to experience a contemporary separation fully in a manner that might facilitate moving toward a resolution of the original grief.

Chapter VII

THE APPLICATION OF FAMILY SYSTEMS THEORY TO CRISIS INTERVENTION

W. Robert Beavers, M.D.

Behavioral research has made important advances toward viewing emotional illness as part of a system within which the disturbed person moves. In years past, the focus was on the individual social deviant— classifying his characteristics, identifying clusters of symptoms, and paying little attention to the interactional aspects of his environment. Gradually emphasis shifted to intrapersonal psychodynamics—not just what was wrong, but why the person behaved differently in terms of his own peculiar personality. Psychiatric theory based on individual psychodynamics remains the cornerstone of the treatment of emotional ills. However, the theoretical base has broadened. First anecdotally, then systematically, families were observed to differ in style and mode of operation, and these differences were correlated with disturbances in their offspring.

The pastoral counselor may find a succinct presentation of family systems theory useful in his work with individuals and families in crisis. Pastors are at the forefront in dealing with human disturbances at family level, and they may sometimes be unsuccessful through failure to consider the particular family matrix in which a person in crisis is embedded.

SYSTEMS THEORY

Observations of families are augmented by consideration of general systems theory. This theoretical framework begins with the concept of *entropy*, a complex term referring to the state of organization and energy in a closed system. In a closed system no energy comes in from outside and everything goes downhill, that is, becomes more entropic. For example, in a world without an external source of energy, life structures disintegrate, and a steady state of maximum entropy results. Life is possible only in an open system. Even a one-celled organism is an open system, receiving energy from the less organized outside world and using it in developing and maintaining structure and flexibility. The miracle of life is possible because of negative entropy (*negentropy*), where available energy is used to develop structure and fight the inexorable downhill pull seen in a closed system.

In living systems, structure with flexibility is optimal. The more an organism develops, the more negentropy is demonstrated. Cells in an organism proliferate, specialize, cooperate, with ever-increasing power to interact with the environment. If one kills a living organism and mounts a section on a slide, he can observe its fabulous structure. That dead organic material is still more negentropic than the material from which it developed, but it has no further ability to adapt. The movement of living systems up the ladder of organization may be conceptualized as movement from chaos through rigidity with some differentiation of parts, to greater and greater coherent structure with flexibility.

This description of the characteristics of an open system as it increases in negentropy corresponds to what is actually seen in family structures, ranging from those defined as severely disturbed to those defined as healthy. For purposes of simplicity and coherence, we can place all family systems on a continuum from the most entropic—those most disorganized and chaotic—to some that are rigid and inept, on to the healthy systems—those most organized and yet flexible. For this purpose we will discuss three general levels of family functioning: the seriously disturbed, the midrange, and the healthy, describing rather consistent characteristics seen in the family patterns of each of these general types. Descriptions of family characteristics at stages along the continuum emphasize the view that most human psychopathology evolves not from a specific, qualitatively different kind of system but as a result of the deficiency of needed qualities along several dimensions of family interaction. This has implications for the effectiveness of efforts to help people during stress.

The two groups at the extremes of this continuum of family functioning will be discussed first since they represent the smallest portion of the minister's counseling load. The midrange family group will be discussed in the last and longest section of the chapter since it is this group from which most of the case load of helpers comes.

THE SEVERELY DISTURBED FAMILY

Table I lists some salient characteristics of the three groups of families arbitrarily defined from the continuum of family systems. The severely disturbed families are poorly organized and poorly differentiated, clinging in a sticky lump, with little vital interchange with the outside world and little change in the family world. Dreams, fantasies, and a studied unawareness take the place of goal-directed, active negotiations between persons. In a community setting, these families are usually seen as queer, odd, strange; their children are shunned by other children; they display peculiar, distancing attitudes and relationships in social groupings. Most significantly, the family members are almost completely unable to separate themselves from one another and invest energy in the outside world.

Members of seriously disturbed families behave much as mutually intimidating members of an illicit gang, checking each other to make certain that no one is out of line. This becomes automatic and family members are truly not aware of how much "group-think" they do and how little respect they pay to individual

---

Table I

TYPES OF FAMILY SYSTEMS

A. *Seriously Disturbed—most entropic*

    1. Family is queer, odd, strange
    2. Lack of individual boundaries
    3. Strong sense of timelessness
    4. Poor parental coalition—a child often powerful

    5. Frequent speaking for others
    6. Unresponsive to one another
    7. Individual choice impossible
    8. Poor task performance

B. *Midrange—rigidly structured*

    1. Autonomy possible, but severely restricted
    2. Man's essential nature seen as evil
    3. Child-rearing seen as a battle for control
    4. Ubiquitous referee dominates family members
    5. Parental coalition either poor, or good by subjugation of one parent
    6. Feeling tone varies from polite to angry or depressed
    7. Scapegoating frequent
    8. Resistant to change, but hope for good change is alive

C. *Healthy—structure with flexibility*

    1. High degree of autonomy
    2. Man's nature seen as neutral or good
    3. Feeling tone positive, frequent laughter
    4. Frequent real encounters, sharing
    5. Extremely open and receptive
    6. Good parental coalition
    7. Power shared, no domination
    8. High task efficiency

---

perception and feeling. Different phrases have been used to describe this characteristic, such as "undifferentiated ego mass," "pseudo-mutuality," "rubber fence," or "mystification." All these terms describe the same phenomenon: the failure of a family to help its offspring develop the autonomy and clear boundaries of self that allow for a coherent identity. Such failure is not passive, but an active conspiracy to avoid coherence and meaning. The process, found most pervasively (but not exclusively) in families who produce children later diagnosed schizophrenic, operates as a cognitive and emotional swamp from which extrication seems impossible. In fact, a reasonable and helpful way to view schizophrenia during adolescence is as a desperate attempt to leave the family's murky, quicksand-filled swamp. The experience of shared meaning is almost absent in these least autonomous families. Negotiation becomes hopeless; the passage of time is obliterated; relationships remain unclear and unchanging.

A young woman describes her timeless family thus:

I lived in absoluteness, my world moved in the slow, unchanging, unquestioned rhythm of a dream. It *was* a dream. Nothing moved in the basic outlines of our existence. Life was as absolute and predictable as a path we had beaten between our house and our grandparent's. Relationships were secure, they were the same when I woke in the morning as they had been when I went to bed the night before. Life was slow then; we lived in a rhythm, but it was not based on time, it was based on direction. We moved in a circle, time belonged to the world, but we belonged to ourselves. We were frozen. I wore that rhythm like a ring around the faithful finger of my life.

The power in such families is usually held (unclearly, of course!) by one parent with an almost nonexistent parental coalition. Quite often there is an obvious parent-child coalition that breaks down generation barriers, parentifying a child and destroying the excluded parent's effectiveness, with his or her subsequent functioning more as a child, a sibling than a parent.

The lack of clear definition of a self and the absence of clear boundaries between individual family members are validated by high frequency with which one person speaks for another—"We all feel just the same about church"; "Sally doesn't really mean to be impolite, she's just tired"; "John, you are not angry at your brother, you're just upset and confused."

These families also have the highest frequency of a person's being ignored by other family members—a father may be so excluded, for example, that he is rendered completely helpless whenever he attempts to join in family deliberation. It is more common, however, that such discriminatory lack of responsiveness is seen in reference to one or more of the children.

Because of the lack of individuation, personal choice that is recognized and accepted is a rare event. Members of these families try to achieve closeness by identical thinking and feeling. Therefore, individuation is tantamount to rejection and exclusion. The children grow up haunted by the impossibility of attaining two goals made incompatible in such a system—being an individual and having acceptance and companionship.

All of us struggle for both of these, even if we have satisfactory early family experiences. Later, we often find social structures frustrating in this respect. Employees cannot "be themselves" around many bosses; housewives cannot express dissident opinions in the PTA without risking social ostracism. Students who point out authoritarianism in the high schools of our democracy risk expulsion. Such frustration, however, is mild compared to the powerful social pressures brought to bear in a family. If one cannot be himself in his family, he is very likely to have no self at all. This sad state of affairs is a result of the rule system of the whole family structure. It is important to remember that no person is victim and another villain, but all are caught up in a nightmare without end.

These families are least productive or efficient when asked by family researchers to accomplish some shared task such as "planning something together." It is so threatening to express any deviant idea or personal opinion that bogging down is inevitable. The group feeling tone is generally apathetic, hopeless, empty, or at times brittle and cynical. Open anger is rare, for that would imply hope of change or extrication, and, of course, genuine joy, warmth, and laughter are absent.

It is this author's view that the seriously disturbed family will adjust to a crisis (such as the death of a family member) in one of two very disparate ways. One, it may actually use the crisis to learn some necessary realities about the family system and the family members. If this occurs, there will be a lengthy period of pain, during which the family will need much assistance from outside helpers. Crisis resolution will not be short because an extensive amount of learning is necessary. The alternative and more frequent method such families use to adapt to stress is to continue to block out reality, preserving the myth that nothing is different. It is likely that the family will seek to bolster this mythology, denying the realities of growth and development, aging and death, through religious concepts, e.g., the loved one has not died, but is present in some other level of living.

Beliefs in life after death are not, of course, necessarily used to blur the realities of loss, but the clearly dysfunctional family may often use such concepts as a denial and as a means of maintaining the family system, maladaptive as it might be. Such concepts help disturbed families continue to live in a murky time-lessness with the bittersweet virtue of such a position —never really encountering each other, but never really losing each other.

The pastoral counselor will usually act as a referring agent in these families if he sees any real hope for change—a crisis dealt with as an opportunity for growth will revolutionize the family system and require much time from probably more than one professional helper.

If a disturbed family is clearly not open to a change in its system, then the minister may be most helpful by seeking only to reduce the symptoms of the crisis. This may be done by his actually supporting the family's usual defensive mechanisms and maneuvers and myths, which, although barriers to individual growth, still hold the family together in some way. In dealing with a death, for example, very often such "religious" concepts as "he is not dead, but sleeping" or "he is still present in spirit" are gratefully used by the family system to deny any real loss or change and per-haps is what they need and will accept at that time.

THE HEALTHY FAMILY

The group at the most adaptive end of the function-ing continuum includes families whose members have no evidence of crippling psychopathology. Knowledge of the factors present in such capable families is cer-tainly incomplete. Studies of healthy families are of recent origin and are few in number as compared to studies of pathological families. Recognizing gaps in our knowledge, we can, however, begin to describe the functioning of family systems that do a reasonably good job in helping infants evolve into successful adults. Table I lists some prominent characteristics of this group. The presence of autonomous and relatively conflict-free interaction is immediately apparent. Parents have a functioning coalition with an accepted degree of power between them, and the children have less power. There is a relatively clear and flexible family rule system. Expression of feeling is frequent and open. Participation in tasks is widely shared. There are no rigid rules regarding who can say what to whom. Interruptions are frequent and are taken lightly, with the speaker comfortably overriding the interruption and finishing his contribution. Family members are not intimidated by any covert, unspoken taboos or prohibitions. Ambivalence is acceptable, and true negotiations are frequent. These families do not demand total agreement; instead they seek and often achieve inventive compromise. In an atmosphere relatively free of intimidation, such disturbing defenses as projection, denial, and blaming are unnecessary and infrequent. Therefore, scapegoating is not seen, since no individual needs to avoid taking personal responsibility for his own feelings, thoughts, and actions. In family groups where individuals have suitable autonomy, a coherent rule system coincides with a tolerance of individuality. An unspoken but strongly held view that people, while responsible for their behavior, can think and feel just about what they wish, removes much of the necessity to control. There is an underlying attitude that man is not essentially evil, but is either neutral or essentially positive in his basic nature. As a result, parenting is seen more as education and relationship than as control and intimidation. Family interaction is generally pleasant, with frequent laughter, disruptions, "inside" remarks, and the effort to accomplish a task seems almost effortless.

Watching videotapes of such families is often like sharing a delightful and exciting adventure as one observes the pleasant, flexible, varying communication network with lively receivers and transmitters. The conversational ball whips back and forth in a sometimes dizzying fashion. In a healthy family system one can be candid, open, and vulnerable. The comprehensive expression of views and feelings by all family members is much more frequent in the healthy family than in any less adaptive group. Generally, deviating opinions are accepted as significant. Devious or heavy-handed efforts to change these opinions are either absent or unsuccessful. These family members are receptive to one another with open acknowledgment of every individual's input into the system.

The family structure is the least authoritarian, the clearest, and the most flexible. The typical healthy family has two parents both powerful within the system. The parents operate in a complementary rather than symmetrical or competitive fashion most of the time. This allows them both to have strength with little rivalry. Since both are considered important, they invite each other's opinions in important decisions of child-raising. The children are less powerful, but their contributions are attended and incorporated in family decisions. As a result, defensive power struggles are not necessary, and family tasks are undertaken with reasonable cooperativeness, good humor, and effectiveness.

Because of the open system with a relatively clear structure and the lack of necessity for intimidation, the myths of healthy families conform relatively closely to observed interactional reality. This is interrelated with these families' acceptance of the inevitable processes of growth and development, aging and death. This the healthy family members do better than any other group. Because of their strong coalition, parents break excessive ties to their own parents. This allows the opportunity to have good generation barriers in their own developing family which is then a very powerful assistance to the developing child in growing and separating from his original family.

However, the demands of living, of facing the emptiness and the realities of aging and death are only partially met by a gratifying husband-wife relationship. In these families, the ability to relate well to people in the outside world, to have meaningful encounters and relationships in the broader environment cannot be overemphasized. These relationships, reaching into the wider community, are sources of energy to the family structure and put life into the system. They are basic to the ability of the parents to accept their own aging and the developing autonomy of their children with equanimity.

Because the system is open to new input, it is able to adapt to changing circumstances even though they may be painful. This group of families is most responsive to crisis intervention and will offer very little resistance to the pastoral counselor's efforts to intervene effectively in crises. The technique and methodology of crisis intervention that is explored in the rest of the book may be used well without fear of serious booby traps or special pitfalls. It is with such essentially healthy families that a genuine desire to help and a respected position in a community will work wonders.

As a pastoral counselor begins to work in crisis intervention, let us hope that he gets a few such healthy systems to work with in the beginning. They are gratifying, and can teach a helper a great deal about being flexible, open, perceptive, and goal-directed, even when stressed by a crisis.

THE MIDRANGE FAMILY

We have described characteristics of family systems at the lower and upper ends of a continuum of functioning. Insight into these families is useful, but they do not constitute the main source of people who seek advice, counseling, or treatment. It is the large group of families in the midrange that supply most of these seekers for help. Research studies surveying large populations indicate that there are more members of families who are emotionally disturbed than there are with no symptoms. Estimates of 66 to 75 percent are common regarding that portion of the public hampered by diagnosable mental illness. Therefore, the rest of this chapter will focus on this group of families, systems which allow the development of a coherent identity in the offspring, but at the expense of much that is possible in human behavior and self-image. These families produce offspring with a modest repertoire of interpersonal skills and a constricted, generally guilt-laden image of the self. Psychiatrists may label products from these families neurotic or give them various behavior disorder labels. These labels are somewhat useful when understood as an attempt to describe the person's characteristically limited behavior patterns in a variety of interpersonal situations that often result in emotional pain and/or failure. The families of both neurotics and those with behavior disorders belong in this midrange classification. They have some significant similarities, but also some very important differences. We will begin by presenting those characteristics held in common by midrange families. Table I, section B provides a list of these for ready reference.

First, and prominently, the development of autonomy is more successful than in the seriously disturbed. Family members are generally clear and relatively unambiguous. That is, as one observes family interaction, there is a reasonably clear idea of where one person leaves off and the next one begins. Personally invasive comments (mind-reading) are rare.

Within rather severe limits, family members take responsibility for their feelings, actions, and thoughts, so that personal choice is possible. And in addition, a greater degree of acknowledgment and responsiveness is found. In short, there is a reluctant but honest acceptance of the reality of separateness: husband from wife, parents from children. This is in sharp contrast to the severely disturbed family, where this acceptance is lacking, and to the healthy family, where this acceptance is not reluctant, but satisfying.

The underlying reason for this reluctance to accept separateness is the pervading view of midrange families that man is essentially evil. His very nature and essential drives are willful and antisocial, and hence there is a never-ceasing effort to control and inhibit oneself, one's spouse, and one's children. (It can be readily seen that this view is one of those beliefs that serves as a *self-fulfilling prophecy*. When people are over-controlled, they tend to try to rebel and this provides "evidence" of the correctness of the assumption.)

Seeing child-raising as a war in the nursery is then

inevitable from this combination of seeing one's family members as separate, evil, willful, and possibly controllable.

The definition of what is good or acceptable in people excludes a great deal of what is essentially human. Anger is usually considered unambivalently bad; sexual feelings rarely are accepted, and even ambivalence (simultaneous positive and negative feeling response to an object, person, or situation) is disapproved. This last prohibition (i.e., good people do not have ambivalence; they hate the bad things and love the right things with nothing in between) is surprisingly destructive of pleasant interaction and peace of mind. This is because ambivalence is an ever-present quality that is at the heart of being human. We humans are born with an infinite capacity to fantasize perfection, but this dream capacity is bound up in a finite, failing mortal who constantly falls short and is in turn let down by others when he expects absolutes.

The midrange family member never allows this essential truth to sink in, however, and failure and finite humanness are often perceived as the willful evil self coming through that must be dealt with quickly and harshly.

In observing the interaction of midrange families, I have the strong impression that an invisible referee is present. This referee is a tyrant that subjugates all the family members and is a peculiarly stupid and insensitive one at that. He has standards of thoughts, behavior, and feelings that are pathetically inadequate to express the reality of needs of both children and adults. (As one result, much of the self must be expressed either in fantasy or illicit behavior rather than realistic interaction with others.)

195

If a member's wishes and behavior coincide with this referee's rules, he may declare himself with impunity, even smugness. Negative declarations such as "I don't feel angry towards you"; "I'm not unhappy"; "I'm not going to act up again" are frequent and much safer than any positive declarations that usually take more individual responsibility than is comfortable. If the individual's expressed feelings or his behavior are not consistent with the referee's rules, he is ruled out-of-line and is considered bad (rather than untutored). It should be noted that the refereeing system does not limit parental control to behavior; discipline also attempts to control the feelings and thoughts. "You're a good boy, you shouldn't feel that way about your sister." "No decent person has thoughts like that." "You must be crazy to think that way." Although the viewpoint of the other is considered a reality, continuing strong attempts are made to bring everyone's inner life into agreement with the referee's rules. The true feelings of individuals very rarely come out openly, spontaneously, and without pain. If the feelings correspond to the law of the magical and ubiquitous referee, they are apt to come out with sanctimoniousness, unctuousness, and an obvious expression of virtue. If the feelings do not conform to what the referee expects, they will probably be hidden or, if unable to be silenced, expressed with a great deal of shame or guilt. The attempt to control by authoritarianism lessens the opportunity for the development of autonomy. Therefore, severe conflict, overt or covert, is inevitable. Openly expressed, the product is unfriendly, competitive interaction and explosive behavior. Hidden and constricted, it produces a depressive, compulsive atmosphere with little spontaneity. This rigidity of family structure devolves into control vested in the hands of one parent or into a continual battle between the two, offering no example of a successful coalition, no model for negotiation and compromise. This leaves the developing children extremely handicapped in later relationships.

This referee may be abstract or personified. In many families it is a "they," the faceless horde of "good" people who have controlled themselves properly, as judged by their neighbors. In others, it is a formal religious code, adhered to with perfectionistic in-humanness. I am seeing more families nowadays who are agnostic or atheistic in orientation who make of science a lawgiver and referee that can thoroughly tyrannize. Frequently the referee is personified, however. A powerful grandparent or dominating father or mother is seen as the spokesman for the referee (a position of power and no responsibility, since the judgments are from what is "right," not one person's arbitrary humanness).

The quality of parental coalition is dependent on dominance-and-submission patterns. If one parent accepts the submissive role and allows the other to be the main interpreter of the referee, then the coalition is good. If neither can accept submission, then the coalition is poor and the family rule system is always up in the air with frequent battles royal in which the children learn to participate and to initiate when a short-term advantage is found. Specific differences in parental coalitions between behavior disorders and neurotic families will be discussed later.

With either type of parental coalition, successful or unsuccessful domination, task efficiency suffers. Negotiation is difficult or perfunctory because of the rigidity of the system. Due to this relative ineptness in nego-

197

tiation, midrange family members show a variety of negative moods: sadness, depression, low-keyed bickering with occasional explosiveness or argumentativeness, with little warmth or joy. Thus these family systems are midrange in feeling tone as well as in child-rearing effectiveness, able to get by, but showing constant evidence of pain. Since unpleasant feeling states are too frequently present in the family, all the members are especially vulnerable to psychiatric disorders such as depressive and anxiety states.

It should be noted, that since control and narrow, rigid rule systems are an intrinsic part of midrange families, scapegoating frequently develops. Scapegoating refers to the selection of a member or members of a group to receive responsibility for all the evil and sins of group members. Optimally, if scapegoating occurs, it will occur outside the family group. This allows all the family to feel comparatively good about themselves in contrast to those "bad" people (the black, the white, the rich, the poor,) who are outside. In observing families of all degrees of health and pathology, I have never seen one that does not use this mechanism to some degree. The scapegoating becomes destructive, however, when it is directed toward family members. If one member is defined as clearly worse than all the rest, this affords an opportunity to place all unacceptable feelings on this family scapegoat. An inevitable result is that growth and change are markedly handicapped, since a plausible explanation for problems is already available without any change on anyone's part.

The midrange family offers choice and identity, but never without guilt and self-doubt. In contrast to severely disturbed families who are almost never able to let their children go, the midrange family members do, reluctantly, separate physically from their parents, leave and develop new families. However, emotional separation does not occur, and a therapist finds these patients still caught up in a frustrating, conflict-ridden relationship with their parents, or conversely, still ineffectually grieving an idealized parent long dead. The product of the midrange family has the ability to find new relationships, but they are similar in style to those he knew in his original family. Therefore, instead of looking for new relationships that are significantly and qualitatively different, the midrange family offspring keeps the memory of mother and/or father burning bright, recreating them in interactions with new people with ingenuity and skill.

Because of the rigid family structure, there is necessarily resistance to fundamental change in the family system or in the individuals present in such a system. But still hope is alive that change does not always signify degeneration and deterioration and that it could be satisfying "if only. . . ." Generally that sentence is left dangling because the referee is much better at demanding obedience than stating what fundamental changes are needed for growth and development.

These characteristics define and limit the midrange family from the severely disturbed and the healthy. But in addition, there are significant, meaningful differences in family rules between neurotic and behavior disorder families. Table II gives a succinct summary of these differences.

First, the two types of midrange families differ in the way they handle the shared belief that man is essentially evil. The neurotic family sees man as evil, but redeemable, if he will only abdicate his true nature. In order to be acceptable to other people, neurotic families believe they must deny large portions of themselves which are seen as destructive. Thereby, they necessarily become well-meaning frauds. In presenting an acceptable self to others, much of their humanity remains hidden. In contrast, the parents who produce character disorders have no hope of redemption through fraudulence. They feel inadequate, inept, and evil, without expectation that they can successfully fool the world. They have less confidence about how they ought to raise children, and less feeling of virtue through successful activities of their own. As a result of these firm beliefs, the family systems are significantly different in rules, attitudes, and expectations.

In the neurotic family one parent is usually dominant, and a successful parental coalition occurs due to the subservience of the other parent. Since rigidity and authoritarianism are considered necessary to maintain a structure with tight control, a negotiated coalition between two important and significant parents cannot occur. When the subservient parent honestly considers

---

Table II

CONTRASTS BETWEEN BEHAVIOR DISORDER AND NEUROTIC FAMILIES

Behavior Disorder	*Neurotic*
Man evil, not redeemable through fraud	Man evil, redeemable through fraud
Use of denial and projection, more open hostile feelings	Use of repression and reaction formation—masking of hostility

Use of referee to blame and attack others (unsuccessful control)	Use of referee to successfully control self and others
More in lower and low-middle socio-economic classes	More in middle and upper socio-economic classes
Excessive use of non-prescription drugs (e.g., alcohol) often seen	Excessive use of prescription (sanctioned) drugs often seen
History of repeated crises	History of few interpersonal crises with dread of nonconformity

---

that the rule of the more dominant spouse is correct, the family system works, especially when the children are small. Children are, in effect, bribed to accept rules by a reward system imposed by the referee. "If you think and feel what you are supposed to, you are good; and if you don't, you are bad. You must always hide your real feelings. When you hide your real feelings, and behave properly, you have the hang of it—you are a successful fraud."

In contrast, the family of the behavior disorder shows no such strong coalition between the parents. Both parents feel an uneasy sense of inadequacy and inability to do what is "right." They habitually and ineffectually battle for control of the children and the determination of family rules. They are not very powerful as parents. Frequently, one or both parents establish illicit coalitions with children. These are never overt, since such coalitions are considered fun but naughty, and the parent who engages in such maneuvering to gain an advantage against the spouse is never able to feel virtuous about it. Children of such a family system grow to adulthood able to maneuver, manipulate, and play one parent against the other, but are extremely doubtful of their own social acceptability.

A second contrast between these two groups pertains to types of psychological defenses. The neurotic family member uses repression of feelings and thoughts forbidden by the referee. Individuals have a narrow range of expressed feelings and may be truly unconscious of many rebellious or angry impulses. Reaction formation is frequently a defensive maneuver. This refers to a reversal of feelings, such as an expression of warmth and tenderness whenever anger threatens to come to consciousness, a pledge of allegiance whenever disloyalty threatens, or protestations of fondness to overcome nearly conscious mistrust.

Behavior disorder families use denial and projection, with individual members appearing oblivious to their own part in interpersonal difficulties. For example, if the father loses his job partly because of absenteeism, he is apt to blame his wife for not encouraging him or the boss for having it in for him. Because all the family feel relatively weak and unable to control themselves or others, they more obviously and openly break the rules of the family referee. Consequently, they are more likely to be surly, uncooperative, and directly hostile, with frequent recourse to blame and attack.

The behavior disorder family member uses a referee or any powerful authority figure to assist him in this blame and attack. The effort is not so much to gain control over others, but to point out their deficiencies and force them to admit to wrongdoing. The neurotic family, on the other hand, uses a referee to control effectively its own members. Power is sought and generally obtained. The difference is related to the underlying views of their own potential. Behavior disorder families see themselves (and man in general) as evil, and have little hope of successfully hiding this. The best they can expect is to point out that other family members are not worth very much either. The neurotic hopes to hide his evil nature and control himself, and he makes every effort to control others.

Excessive use of nonprescription drugs (the most common example of such drugs is still alcohol) is frequent in the family of the behavior disorder. This is a part of his identity as a bad person, and he does not hope for approval from authorities. Instead he accepts that pleasure is found in the illicit, attempts to enjoy his hidden activity, but always expects to be found out. The family of the neurotic is quite different in this respect. Abuse is usually of prescribed drugs such as tranquilizers, amphetamines, and sleeping medications which are considered to be acceptable because an authority figure has administered them. Heavy use of alcohol is almost never seen in a family of the neurotic except when the structure is deteriorated and hopelessness has run rampant through the whole family system.

In the family of the behavior disorder type, one finds a history of repeated interpersonal crises that serve to maintain the equilibrium of the family system itself. Children run away from home, not in order to leave, but to dramatize that a parent has a lack of love or responsible behavior. A parent will retreat into drunkenness, hoping to make others feel guilty and responsible. Jobs are thrown away, not in an attempt to go to something better, but as punishment for a family member or an authority figure who is thought to be unjust and insensitive. Families of neurotics, however, have very few interpersonal crises *of this nature* because they are concerned with maintaining social status. Fear of what others will think generally produces pain within these individuals, but few flamboyant crisis events.

Although counselors may encounter families in which all members operate in either a behavior disorder or neurotic style, most families are not pure, unmixed types. For example, there are families with some members operating in control-oriented, duty-bound, and socially proper and powerful roles, with others in the same family defined as childlike, willful, and able to use only the control methods of the helpless as described in the behavior disorder family section. That is to say, in order to be as alert as possible to the various patterns family members present, the pastoral counselor will need to be aware of the characteristic behavior disorder and neurotic patterns and realize that they can be mixed in a single family.

Two fairly common configurations in which these two patterns are mixed are as follows:

The *hysteric-compulsive match* is a family pattern in which one parent, usually the male, possesses the characteristics of the neurotic family style. He controls his emotions, he is responsible, he must never have any feelings that are inappropriate as judged by the referee, and he tries at all costs to avoid flamboyant interpersonal crises. The other parent, usually the female, follows the rule system seen in the behavior disorder families, considering herself evil and not redeemable, relatively powerless, needful of an authority figure to control her, yet always trying to evade that control, inclined to use the helplessness to control others by getting into crises, attempting to show that the spouse is not truly filled with Christian love, not truly duty-bound, but rather is a fraud, no better than anyone else.

A second pattern of mixed types is a family with a well-delineated scapegoat where both mother and father, brothers and sisters operate in the characteristic neurotic style. The notable exception is the one child who is defined (and accepts himself) as possessing all the evil qualities that the others successfully hide from themselves and others. He, and only he, will behave according to the behavior disorder family rules since everything is upside down for him because of the peculiar reverse definition that a neurotic family gives the scapegoated member. It should be noted that the mixture comes only from a predominately neurotic family style since the behavior disorder family acts much as if all are scapegoated with no consistent agreement as to who is really the bad one!

Table III lists some special problems found in the family systems when a pastoral counselor engages in crisis work. Family members of the behavior disorder group generally mistrust words and have little faith in the usefulness of verbal statements by the counselor. They are strongly action-oriented, and expect a useful authority figure to *do* something rather than to discuss solutions. In marked contrast, the neurotic family sees words as somewhat magical. Lifelong training produces "I'm sorry" or "please" and often those words have been more important than anything that has been done. Fearful of action and enamored of words, the neurotic family member is prone to immobilization from indeci-

Table III

SPECIAL PROBLEMS IN CRISIS WORK WITH MIDRANGE FAMILIES

Behavior Disorder	*Neurotic*
Talking mistrusted	Words are magic
Action-oriented	Immobilization, indecision common
Fear of referee; superficial compliance or open defiance	Wish to please—to control referee by being nice
May run away before real encounter	Tending to "settle in" and have helper stuck
May use authority as a club over another family member	May use authority as club on oneself, convert suggestions into "shoulds" and "oughts"

SPECIAL LEARNING MOST URGENTLY NEEDED

Behavior Disorder	*Neurotic*
Awareness of one's effect on others and of others' limits	Awareness of one's finiteness and limits, and of others' powers to help

sion. He mistrusts action on his part (or for that matter on the part of the authority). Intervention in crisis can become bogged down with wordiness.

Since the behavior disorder family member fears the ever-present referee, he is most likely to transfer his fear to the pastoral counselor who is trying to intervene in his behalf. The counselor may find either superficial compliance or open defiance and direct hostility. The superficial compliance is in terms of mere lip service designed to placate the counselor. This is a particularly sore point for many counselors who are accustomed to having their words heeded.

The individual in a neurotic family has a strong wish to please. He has learned that he can seduce authorities if he follows the rules, and he will attempt to do so. The problem here for the counselor is that the client will attempt to control the authority figure by such slavish conformity. The underlying bargain is that "I am doing exactly what you say, and therefore you will be forced to promise me good results."

A big danger with the behavior disorder family member is that he may run away before the intervener can develop any real relationship and have a true encounter with his client. On the other hand, the neurotic family member has a strong tendency to settle in and to be a dependent rule-follower that gets in a sticky, continuous, frustrating interaction with the counselor. What starts as an attempt to deal neatly and cleanly in an acute crisis situation can become a life's work.

It may be useful to point out that the behavior disorder family member regularly uses authority as a club to assist him in the never-ceasing games of blame and attack. The pastoral counselor may unwittingly be drawn into a family brawl by such efforts on the part of his client. For example, a wife, tired of verbal abuse from her husband, threatens suicide and checks into a local motel. She calls her minister and informs him of her mental state, and he visits her with crisis intervention in mind. He will need to be very careful not to be set up as the authoritative judge who condemns the bad husband. A visit to the whole family may be in order with an eye to presenting himself as a fair and understanding person rather than a missile to be used in the attack on a spouse.

This is a likely danger since the family member is not used to being effective in dealing with others, and will tend to use the counselor as a club rather than as a resource to obtain more personal power.

In contrast, the neurotic family member often uses authority to club himself. He attempts to convert suggestions of the counselor into "shoulds" and "oughts," rules that he must follow. When he cannot, or will not, follow these rules he tortures himself with these suggestions, rather than using them to work out his difficulty.

This tends to increase the degree of depression found in a client, and is a real pitfall to avoid when attempting to help. I have found two practices most useful to me in reducing this unfortunate tendency of neurotic family members. One, I avoid the use of "shoulds" and "oughts" like the plague, and when they crop up I defuse them by "finishing out the sentence." "You should confront your husband *if you wish to cut down the distance between you.*" "You ought to go back to school *if you are certain you want to finish college.*" Second, even though I avoid the words, the programmed neurotic will use them. I then encourage him to finish out the sentence which converts referee demands into possibilities for choice and decision.

Let us use Table II now in an imaginary crisis and see how a placement of the person in trouble into one of the two categories might be useful.

The wife referred to above has called a minister telling him of her suicidal wishes and of her decision to take a motel room. She is excited, angry, with slightly slurred speech. When the counselor arrives he finds a half-empty bourbon bottle and a woman expressing great anger toward her husband. When asked, she states that such intense breaks with him have been relatively frequent. She wants her husband to change quickly and completely and bring his paycheck home and offer her more repect. A crisis? Of course. But a crisis consistent with and related to a characteristic family pattern.

In contrast, let us suppose that the wife calling the minister was restrained, tense, with a slightly slurred speech. When the counselor arrives he notes a half-empty prescription bottle of Librium and a woman saying she cannot go on. She has no one to turn to and suicide seems attractive. She refuses to blame her husband and instead speaks of his fine qualities. She realizes that it is her failure to make the marriage work, and this is the first time she has ever made such a miserable destructive move as this which will disrupt and disturb the whole family.

Another crisis, to be sure, with a markedly different personality, family structure, and pitfalls to avoid. It is one that has more urgency, since it is against the usual family pattern rather than consistent with it.

A general, overriding rule for those two contrasting types of sane but limited people is seen at the bottom of Table III. The behavior disorder family member is only marginally aware of the effect of his own being, his own actions on others. He sees himself as a tiny child surrounded by giants. He, therefore, is equally unaware of other people's limits and frailties. Often then, he will behave outrageously, truly unaware of the pain and disappointment of others who depend on him. He is apt to believe that when someone he needs lets him down it is because of willfulness, not ineptness. He says of his loved ones, "They really could if they would, if I could only force them."

It is most useful for the counselor to help the client increase his awareness of his potential for power, for effectiveness. "I am significant and potentially effective" is a needed but very muted theme.

In contrast, the neurotic family member desperately needs awareness of his own finiteness and his own limits in order to avoid the overwhelming sense of guilt that often produces continued, unabated depression or suicidal wishes. He is likely to overlook other people's power to help him in his difficulty because he considers that he should do it for himself. This view that he should take care of his own problems or die is not any drive toward growth, development, or autonomy, of course. It is made up of the old family rules: one is either acceptable or pariah; ugly, mean feelings betray a bad person. His is a very tough dilemma. He cannot solve his own problems, and he cannot expose his true self to another because he would be properly rejected. Such a person needs more knowledge of the reality and acceptability of human ineptness and finiteness and the possibility of being acceptable without being a fraud.

It is hoped that this description of different types of family symptoms will aid the pastoral counselor in his efforts to intervene successfully in personal crisis. We all come from family systems and continue to have past or present family rules extremely important in understanding or predicting our behavior. It is hoped that being forewarned is to be forearmed.

Chapter VIII

THE MINISTER
AND DIVORCE CRISES

Richard A. Hunt, Ph.D.

In this volume crisis has been defined as a situation or circumstance in which a major, often sudden, change has occurred that makes an intensive impact upon the usual life-style of an individual or family, the individuals involved feel anxious, overwhelmed, and to some extent unable to cope constructively with the changed circumstances; and a revised solution to the situation is required in a relatively short period of time. Whether divorce can be considered a crisis, or a series of crises, depends upon the perspectives of both the individuals involved and the minister who is offering pastoral care and counseling to them. In our United States culture, perhaps the majority of persons consider divorce at least as an unwelcome occurrence and at most as a major catastrophe from which recovery is never complete. Although there may be a few persons who consider divorce to be just one more event in life with no crisis dimensions, even this interpretation may be a defensive reaction to the deeper changes that divorce inevitably requires.

SOME THEORETICAL PERSPECTIVES ON DIVORCE

Before considering the actual work of pastoral care and counseling with persons in a divorce crisis, it will be helpful to consider the minister's own approach to divorce. There are at least five perspectives which should be examined by the minister as bases for counseling with persons in a divorce crisis. These are demographic, legal, theological, psychological, and personal perspectives.

Demographic

There are misleading interpretations of demographic trends in the United States which some writers use to imply that the institution of marriage is collapsing about us and divorce is of epidemic proportions that threaten to exterminate marriage and the family within a very brief time. For example, the ratio of marriages registered to divorces granted in a particular year and in a specific geographical area does not give a true picture of the current marriage and divorce rates. A pastor who has just seen three of the supposedly stable couples in his congregation obtain divorces, or who has had five of the eight most recent couples with whom he has counseled finally end in divorce, is tempted to assume that we have a crisis of divorce in the entire society.

A more useful statistic is the ratio of divorces per one thousand population. Bernard has provided a careful analysis of recent divorce trends.[1] Except for the post-World–War-II peak in 1946, the rate has been

[1] Jessie Bernard, "Present Demographic Trends and Structural Outcome in Family Life Today," in *Marriage and Family Counseling*, James A. Peterson, ed. (New York: Association Press, 1968).

rising only very slightly since 1920, fluctuating between six and ten divorces per one thousand married female population of fifteen years of age and over. This is a rate of 1 percent of existing marriages which end in divorce each year. The improvement of accurate reporting of divorce statistics and the trend toward easier legal proceedings for divorce may constitute two primary reasons for the apparent slight increase in divorce rates over the past fifty years.

Although an overall average divorce rate may be calculated, this represents a combination of divorce rates, which vary considerably in different parts of the United States, with different ages, and with many other factors. The percentage of marriages that end in divorce is highest (a peak of approximately 6 to 8 percent) during the first four years of marriage and shows a gradual decline from 4 to less than 1 percent between the fifth and thirtieth years of marriage duration. Those who have divorced previously are two to three times as likely to divorce again. From 50 to 75 percent of marriages which occur with one or both partners under age eighteen end in divorce.[2] Those persons with similarity of background, to some extent expressed in religious similarity, have divorce rates that are much lower than those in religiously mixed marriages or with no religious background.[3]

Legal

Technically, divorce is a legal term that refers to the termination of a marriage contract. In these terms, marriage is a civil contract between two individuals, but

[2] Paul H. Landis, *Making the Most of Marriage* (New York: Appleton-Century-Crofts, 1970), pp. 641-66, 310.
[3] Richard H. Klemer, *Marriage and Family Relationships* (New York: Harper & Row, 1970), p. 102.

differing from ordinary contracts in several ways.[4] The process of the dissolution of the marriage contract may be relatively simple, if there is no court contest and if children or property settlements are not involved. Where divorce proceedings are complicated by legal charges and countercharges, battles about child custody or monetary settlements, then the litigation may itself produce secondary crises in addition to the primary emotional reactions to the divorce.

Theological

There is a rather wide range of theological interpretations of divorce which in turn depend upon one's theological and philosophical assumptions about marriage. Hobbs has summarized some of the biblical materials which relate to marriage, although one might disagree with his suggested style of marriage.[5] Perhaps the primary scripture which specifically mentions divorce is Mark 10:2-12 and its parallels in Matthew 5:31-32; 19:3-11, which is set in juxtaposition with Deuteronomy 24:1-4 as one of the tests of the relation between the old Mosaic legalism and Jesus' teachings about the higher righteousness of grace and love as applied in the context of the early gentile Christians living in the Roman Empire. A brief and insightful analysis of Jesus' teachings on marriage and the family is provided by Branscomb[6] and by Bailey.[7]

[4] J. T. Landis and M. G. Landis, *Building a Successful Marriage*, 5th ed. (Englewood Cliffs, N. J.: Prentice-Hall, 1968).

[5] E. C. Hobbs, "An Alternate Model from a Theological Perspective," in *The Family in Search of a Future*, H. A. Otto, ed. (New York: Appleton-Century-Crofts, 1970), pp. 25-41.

[6] B. Harvie Branscomb, *The Teachings of Jesus* (Nashville: Abingdon Press, 1931).

[7] Derrick S. Bailey, *The Mystery of Love and Marriage* (London: SCM Press, 1952).

It seems clear that the intention of Jesus regarding marriage was that the two persons who marry are to remain together for life. In this sense marriage is considered to be an unconditional heterosexual union, and divorce is absolutely out of the question.[8] Although some Christian traditions have applied this teaching literally, thus refusing to recognize divorce (except for adultery), other interpreters assume that the original purpose of this teaching of Jesus was to illustrate again that human beings are already sinners who do what they want, not what God intends, and therefore salvation must come by God's grace, not by reason of the way one has lived.

As a couple enters marriage, the typical Christian wedding ceremony attempts to clarify the intention of each partner to continue with the mate regardless of the circumstances or consequences. This is clearly a commitment to continue together in the marriage without any reservations. It has the possibility of being the solid foundation upon which a couple can give and receive care and acceptability and in the context of which all types of feelings, both positive and negative, can be shared, examined, and utilized in mutual growth and fulfillment.

What is the theological understanding, however, of the couple who, regardless of their intentions at marriage, now, after months and years of married life together, are seriously considering divorce, or perhaps are now divorced? In the New Testament there is abundant emphasis upon grace, forgiveness, restoration, and the possibility of a new decision and commitment to life which is available to every person. In their initial ap-

[8] Rudolf Bultmann, *Theology of the New Testament*, Vols. I, II (New York: Charles Scribner's Sons, 1951, 1955).

proach to marriage, the emphasis is upon complete commitment to make the marriage work for both spouses in the achievement of growth as individuals and to share this fullness with others. When a couple is involved in some aspect of divorce, the changed perspective is based upon what *is*, not what *ought to have been*. There may be some marriage situations in which, given only two alternatives of either continued quarreling and misery or divorce, the divorce is the better of the two decisions. From the perspective of grace, God continues to accept the persons involved, whether they continue in the marriage, divorce, separate, or remarry. Therefore, the crisis of divorce can be accepted as an opportunity for renewal in which each participant learns anew of the pervasiveness of human sin in relation to God and the ways in which individuals are accepted by God. On this basis of unconditional acceptance of each person by God, each individual is then freed to examine his or her own patterns of behavior and interaction, learn from them, and utilize this information for growth and for resolving the divorce crises in the best ways possible.

Personal

Your approach as a minister to the crisis of divorce depends partly upon your own personal experiences in your childhood family, your marriage, and your current family life-style. If neither you nor your relatives have ever personally experienced divorce, you may find it difficult to allow an individual whom you are counseling to make the decision for it. You may feel that the couple just has not tried hard enough to resolve the issues (since *you* have been successful in similar prob-

lems), or that one or both spouses now have the opportunity to escape from each other (which you at
times would like to have had, were it not for being a
clergyman). Or you may experience other subtle feelings
of resentment, hostility, or perhaps anxiety which the
presence of divorce may elicit in you as a person. How
do you really, down deep, feel about your own marriage and family? How do you personally look at
divorce? To be effective in the crisis of divorce with
counselees, you must examine carefully your own very
personal, sometimes suppressed, feelings about your
own family situation.

If you have experienced divorce, either personally or
through a close relative, you may bring other types of
personal feelings to the divorce situation of persons
with whom you work as a pastoral counselor. You may
encourage an easy divorce prematurely, thus preventing the counselees from finding for themselves their
own decision concerning their marriage. It may be possible that your own guilt about a divorce in your past
may combine with a parishioner's divorce crisis to
produce anxiety in you and prevent your functioning
at maximum levels with him or her. On the other hand,
having experienced a divorce and worked through the
attendant feelings in a satisfactory manner, you may be
more sensitive to the dilemmas and uncertainties that
the divorce process can bring to individuals who seem
relatively mature and stable.

Whatever your personal situation, it is important
that you can examine your own positive and negative
thoughts and feelings concerning divorce. Only in this
way can you become a flexible, free person who can
interact constructively with the individuals in a divorce
crisis. The possibilities of counselee growth depend

217

heavily upon the level of your own personal empathy, respect, genuineness, and concreteness in relation to the individuals in a divorce crisis.

Psychological

There is little, if any, relation between the legal grounds for divorce and the psychological dynamics that lead two mates to go their separate ways. Although cruelty, neglect, and indignities account for approximately 75 percent of the legal reasons for divorce,[9] the conscious personal reasons behind these stated legal reasons are typically financial tensions, dissatisfaction, alcoholism, adultery, and other forms of dysfunctional behavior. Underlying these conscious and rather specific reasons are motivational and emotional factors which are expressed in these behavioral forms. The demographic (sociological), legal, theological, and personal perspectives form the context within which the psychological aspects of divorce are set.

A broad understanding of various aspects of divorce will be assisted by reference to Haussman and Guitar and to Bohannon.[10]

THE PSYCHOLOGICAL PROCESS OF DIVORCE

Divorce is not a one-time decision. It is a process that begins months before the initiation of the legal process and continues far beyond the final decree. In one study of 425 couples, only about 20 percent had

[9] Landis, *Making the Most of Marriage*, p. 646.
[10] Florence Haussman and Mary Ann Guitar, *The Divorce Handbook* (New York: G. P. Putnam's Sons, 1960); Paul Bohannan, ed., *Divorce and After* (Garden City, N. Y.: Doubleday & Co., 1970).

secured their divorce decree within eleven months or less from the time they first seriously considered the action, while over 50 percent had seriously considered divorce for one to three years prior to the granting of the decree.[11]

The process of divorce can be considered as a series of six stages, or steps. At each step the minister has unique tasks to accomplish with the persons involved. The progression is not inevitable, since at any crisis point the individuals may be able to resolve the problems and continue together.

Stage One

The first step and possible preliminary crisis relating to divorce occurs when one or both spouses have vague feelings that everything is not quite right or happy in the marriage. Although no specific instances of failure may be identified clearly, there is a general feeling of discomfort. Initially individuals do not express these feelings but continue to hold them within themselves, thus creating secondary or additional anxiety about whether the mate knows that something is wrong. This discomfort may be related to the real but consciously forgotten expectations of parents, mate, or self.[12] Due to these feelings of anxiety, a variety of defense reactions may occur, such as disturbances of sexual functioning or psychosomatic disorders. Some persons may return to behavior patterns that were appropriate at an earlier age (regression), refuse to talk about their feelings (withdrawal), or explain them away (rationalization).

[11] William J. Goode, *After Divorce* (New York: Free Press of Glencoe, 1956), p. 137.

[12] Rubin Blanck and Gertrude Blanck, *Marriage and Personal Development* (New York: Columbia University Press, 1968).

The minister is not likely to see many persons during this first stage of the divorce process. Those whom he does see will probably come with presenting complaints which seem quite unrelated to any consideration of divorce. The minister can be most effective at this point by assisting the individual, or perhaps couple, to give expression to the uneasiness and ambiguities and thus clarify the situation. The counselor certainly would *not* want to greet these complaints with the simple assessment, "You are thinking about getting a divorce." This would probably only make it more difficult for the parishioner to talk with the pastor. In many instances the most active step the pastor can take at this point is to make his or her counseling services available and known to the individuals with these vague feelings of discomfort.

Some parishioners may request reading resources. A brief pamphlet by Ogg is very helpful. More extensive popular presentations are provided by Cantor, Kling, and Callahan.[13]

Stage Two

One spouse decides that the discrepancy between overt behavior and underlying feelings is too great to be ignored. At this point divorce as one solution may begin to be considered. Other possible solutions, such as attempts at changing oneself or the mate, changing

[13] Elizabeth Ogg, *Divorce* (New York: Public Affairs Pamphlet #380, 1965); Donald J. Cantor, *Escape from Marriage* (New York: William Morrow & Co., 1971); Samuel G. Kling, *The Complete Guide to Divorce* (New York: Random House, 1963); P. J. T. Callahan, *The Law of Separation and Divorce* (Dobbs Ferry, N. Y.: Oceana Publications, 1970).

jobs, residence, or other externals may also be sought to reduce the apparent discrepancy between what one desires (expectations) and what seems to be happening (the perceived situation). A definite decision about divorce has not been made, but the individual may suggest that "things can't go on as they are." This feeling may be expressed to the mate, perhaps to friends or relatives or to the minister.

The individual's awareness of his own judgment that things cannot continue as they are may precipitate a variety of secondary reactive feelings, such as guilt, panic, anxiety, withdrawal, or aggression. If the individual comes at this time to the minister-counselor, the primary task of the pastor, in addition to usual principles of counseling, is to allow the individual freedom to explore his or her basic feelings and thoughts about possible termination of the marriage, alternatives to termination, and secondary feelings relating to this decision. It is at this point that the individual first begins to consider the details of divorce. The counselee may be asking questions such as these: "Who will have custody of the children?" "How can I explain the breakup to my relatives and friends?" "How will I support myself financially?" What will others think of me?" "What are the relative advantages and disadvantages of divorce as compared to the difficulty and pain of staying together?" Even these questions may precipitate panic, depending upon the individual's sense of self-sufficiency. The person who is no longer closely tied to relatives may not care very much about their reactions, while another person who has several close relatives who have divorced may almost expect that divorce is the typical way that marriage ends. The woman with no job or career experience may be quite fearful that she cannot survive as a divorced person. The man whose job efficiency and possible promotion may depend in part upon maintaining the appearance of a successful marriage may also be anxious about the negative consequences of divorce on his goals. These are the beginnings of what might be called secondary crises, which are often the spin-off from the central divorce decision.

Stage Three

There may be tentative or genuine efforts at reconciliation by one or perhaps both spouses. One of two primary courses will develop at this point. If the reconciliation efforts are successful, then the consideration of divorce is either eliminated or at least pushed into the background so long as things continue to improve between the couple. If efforts toward marriage improvement are not successful, then the decision to divorce becomes clear and definite, with both spouses knowing of the decision. Typically this decision is then announced by each spouse to close friends, relatives, and the minister.

The action that the minister may take at this step will depend upon his or her relation to the couple and the types of reconciliation efforts they are making. If the minister hears of the decision from others but not from the persons involved, then as one aspect of active pastoral care, he may approach one or both spouses with an expression of concern and an offer of his availability for counseling. For example, in a visit to one or both spouses, or at another appropriate time, the pastor may say, "I have heard that you are considering divorce. For most persons, this is a difficult time. I do not assume that you should either stay married or divorce, but I am available for you to discuss any matters with me that might help you to arrive at a satisfying solution for you and your family. If you would prefer, I can suggest other counselors who could also provide the opportunity for you to explore the issues without telling you what you should do, since that is your decision." If the individual accepts the pastor's invitation, then the situation becomes one in which the individual has told the pastor of the decision.

When the individual has come to the minister to discuss divorce, general principles of counseling are basic. If the couple is sufficiently motivated to attempt reconciliation efforts, then the situation develops into a marriage counseling process, requiring all the specialized skills for that process. If these efforts at improving the marriage are successful, then divorce is avoided, and the marriage may be changed into a success. A most helpful reference for the minister is Stewart. More technical references are available, such as Silverman, Ard and Ard, and Satir.[14]

If it seems that divorce is the most satisfactory solution to the marriage difficulties, then it is important for the minister to accept the freedom of the spouses to make this decision, without in any way condemning or otherwise rejecting them for it. Instead, the pastor may assist them to raise important questions and confront the crisis aspects of the divorce. As in premarital counseling, this predivorce counseling should enable

[14] Charles Stewart, *The Minister as Marriage Counselor*, rev. ed. (Nashville: Abingdon Press, 1970); H. L. Silverman, ed., *Marital Counseling* (Springfield, Ill.: Charles C. Thomas, 1967); B. N. Ard and C. Ard, eds., *Handbook of Marriage Counseling* (Palo Alto: Science and Behavior Books, 1969); Virginia Satir, *Conjoint Family Therapy* (Palo Alto: Science and Behavior Books, 1964).

the spouse or spouses to (a) express feelings of ambivalence and hostility which may surround the decision, (b) separate real from imagined or misinformed problems, and (c) find solutions to practical problems relating to the decision. Some of these practical issues include when the individuals intend to separate (if still together), how family income and property will be divided, who will care for children, and how living arrangements will be changed. Some decisions may be final, and others may be temporary with further review at a later time, such as after the divorce becomes final. There is also the matter of the legal aspects of the divorce. The minister's predivorce counseling will focus upon the individuals' feelings and upon securing appropriate expert help in areas that are not within his own competence. Legal technicalities are properly the responsibility of an attorney. The minister may provide appropriate referral assistance in securing qualified counsel for questions and information about these aspects of divorce.

Stage Four

After the decision to divorce, an attorney is contacted and legal proceedings are begun. During this interim of several weeks or months between initiation of the legal process and the final decree, there is usually the need by one or both parties to examine further their personal reasons for divorce and to finalize postdivorce arrangements. Some spouses may entertain hope that a last minute breakthrough may occur which will make the divorce unnecessary. During this time the first impact of the reality and finality of the divorce will come to the individuals involved. The pastor needs at least to

224

remain in contact with them in order to provide them the opportunity to express these anxieties and to discuss other matters relating to the action. Some persons will experience a major crisis when the realness of the action is experienced. If the pastor is sought for counseling, the basic principles of crisis counseling will apply. What resources and strengths does the individual have? Clarification of the issues is important. What hidden feelings and anxieties have been brought into consciousness as a result of anticipation of divorce? What current conflicts and perhaps bitterness is developing between the spouses? Regardless of the date for the legal termination of the marriage, the psychological divorce usually occurs earlier and precipitates the need to work through feelings of rejection, depression, anxiety, guilt, hostility, loss of self-esteem, and perhaps increased meaninglessness of life.

In other instances, however, the psychological divorce may bring feelings of relief, renewal, and increased self-esteem as the person experiences release from a miserable or intolerable marriage situation. These may be the basic responses to the situation, or sometimes they may be defensive denial of the reality of the loss.

In most persons a mixture of pain and relief will result from the psychological realization of the divorce. Even if all details of postdivorce plans seem appropriate and in order, there may be crisis aspects of the psychological divorce stage. Dependency needs of the individual may increase, which means that person may want you as pastor to be available any time to do special favors. Without unwittingly becoming caught in this web, the pastor will be needed by the individuals to provide steady support in the inner reorientation process of subjective acceptance of the divorce.

Stage Five

The final divorce decree is granted by the court. In some states and some cases, an interlocutory (temporary) decree is granted which provides a waiting period before the divorced may remarry. As part of the decree, postdivorce living arrangements, income distribution, property settlements, and related conditions become final and in force.

Although this date is commonly considered as the change of status from married to divorced, its psychological meaning depends upon the extent to which the individuals have become emotionally divorced before the issuance of the final decree. If they have worked through the crisis of psychological divorce itself, as described in stage four, then the next step (stage six) of readjustment to being single begins immediately. If the psychological reality of divorce first becomes real with the final formal decree, then the minister will do the crisis intervention and counseling described in stage four at this time before the individuals can begin to work on the readjustment phase.

Stage Six

After divorce, the initial period of readjustment to being single again must be faced. This may have begun earlier, but often may be prevented by legal complexities. For example, some individuals may assume that they are already single again and can date others before the divorce is complete and final. In a contested divorce, the spouse who is seeking the divorce may have had to live in a carefully proscribed manner to avoid giving possible evidence to the accusing mate that would prevent the divorce action. In other instances, however, the actual date of the decree may make little additional change in the individuals' daily routine. In every case there will be adjustments to new living conditions, possible renewed dating, and other changes that result from the divorce.[15]

Try as one may, there is no way in which an individual can return to the same type of single status which he had prior to the marriage. Even if all legal and community distinctions of divorced from single status were eliminated, the divorced person is psychologically in a different situation from either the single, married, or widowed person. The readjustments of the divorced person will typically take the form of either bereavement and grief processes or feelings of genuine relief from tensions, although both trends may be present in the same individual. Overtones of these feelings will continue with the person throughout life, although the primary divorce readjustment will typically require approximately a year to complete.

The exact combination of feelings about postdivorce adjustments will depend upon the individual's perception and evaluation of the marriage situation. If the person's marriage was filled with tension, uncertainty, fear, and other hurtful (ego-deflating) feelings, then the postdivorce adjustment period will probably be seen as a welcome relief and an opportunity to begin living again. Even with this more positive view, the person may still seek to understand what went wrong in the marriage, to what extent he caused the problems, and how to avoid getting into a similar situation. The return to dating other persons may also bring feelings of

[15] Morton M. Hunt, *The World of the Formerly Married* (New York: McGraw-Hill Book Co., 1966).

uncertainty and an intensified carefulness to avoid becoming enmeshed in such a painful relationship.

Probably most persons with this positive evaluation of their divorce will be unlikely to seek counseling. In those instances when these persons do seek counseling, the primary focus must be upon the actual adjustments to current situations in the context of having had an unhappy marriage experience. To what extent does the individual realize that the miserable marriage was a product of the two persons together? In what ways is the individual now changing his behavior patterns in order to attract a different type of person, if remarriage is the goal? With what groups of persons in similar circumstances does the individual associate? Are these groups likely to provide wholesome and genuine sources of self-esteem for the individual? What generalized attitudes toward men and women does the individual have that may distort the perspective he has concerning involvement with the other sex? These and related specialized areas need to be explored as part of the readjustment counseling.

At some point there must be a fully conscious psychological acceptance of the reality of the changes related to divorce. In some persons, this occurs before the divorce decree, in others within the first few months after the final decree. If not at these points, then the individual who seems overly accepting, elated, and unrealistically happy (euphoric) about the new freedom of the divorce situation may be covering up (suppressing) his painful feelings about the termination of the marriage. Facing these deeper feelings may be prevented if the individual should marry shortly after divorce. Other individuals may experience the shock of divorce several months after the decree when they have had difficulty in meeting new friends, resolving financial problems, or handling other aspects of the postdivorce life-style.

In some individuals, the delayed impact of the crisis may precipitate more serious defensive patterns. Some persons may begin to act as they did at earlier stages of life, responding in ways which would have been appropriate then, but not now (regression). These might include inappropriate humor or giddiness, disorganized planning, treating the pastor as a parent, and expecting others to take all the responsibility for any unpleasant situation that arises. Other persons may act out sexual or aggressive feelings. For example, a woman may dress and talk seductively in her contacts with a male pastor. Another typical acting-out behavior is the individual who is mad at the pastor for supposed minor injustices or failures. Depression may be another way in which the individual responds to the crisis. Usually depression is hostility which the individual turns inward on himself because he is afraid to express it openly toward the original target of the anger. In other instances, an individual may displace hostility by becoming angry without apparent reason with an innocent person. For example, a woman may exhibit hostile behavior toward her son who in some way reminds her of her ex-husband with whom she is angry but toward whom she cannot express that anger directly.

Frequently bereavement and grief processes will be a part of the postdivorce adjustment. These may follow typical patterns of bereavement and grief.[16] The major difference is that the mate *is* lost but is *not* actually gone. The ex-spouses may continue to see each other

[16] Switzer, *The Dynamics of Grief.*

because of visitation rights for children, financial involvements, mutual friends, or even accidental meetings.

The spouse who did not want the marriage to end may have considerable hostility directed toward the ex-mate, the ex-mate's friends, and possible romantic acquaintances, which is often displaced onto others (family, children, friends), or turned inward to appear in the form of guilt and depression. One task in the counseling situation is to allow the individual to acknowledge this hostility and dispose of it in a healthy manner through forgiveness, changing the situation, and changing one's own self-evaluation.

Dealing with this hostility may be part of the grief work related to divorce adjustment. The grief results from the sense of losing a very valuable and important person in one's life. To compound the grief further, the loss was not due to physical death. Physical death often is interpreted to mean that the loss occurred, and there was really nothing more the surviving spouse could have done to prevent it. If the divorce is interpreted by the individual in this way, that is, as a real event that cannot be changed in any way (thus the divorce is as final as death), then grief over the loss may be expressed, the loss acknowledged openly, and the individual may move on to reconstruct life from this point. To the extent that an individual interprets the divorce as inevitable, the pastor should not seek to change this interpretation, although he may feel that no divorce is inevitable if both parties genuinely work at resolving the problems.

The most difficult grief, however, is the situation in which the loss has occurred, yet the bereaved person

230

continues to have unrealistic hope that the loss is not final, and the ex-spouse will return. This may lead to continuous neurotic attempts to entice, harass, cajole, or otherwise seek the return of the ex-spouse because of the individual's unresolved dependency needs. Another form of this grief may occur in the effort of the individual to find a new spouse who is either identical to the former mate or quite opposite. In either instance, the adjustment behavior is being controlled by the unresolved grief relating to the lost partner.

If the individual comes for counseling at this point, then the task of counseling is to assist the individual to identify his hostility and grief reactions and to examine how these reactions are related to loss situations that happened to the person earlier (such as moving away from one's childhood home, loss of relatives, failure at one's job, education, or other goals). In this way the painful edge of the crisis is blunted and the individual can then proceed toward more realistic post-divorce adjustments.

If the individual displays these grief reactions, yet does not come for counseling, then the pastor may take the initiative through a pastoral contact of some type. For example, he may suggest the possibility of counseling by stating, "It has been several weeks (or months) since your divorce. This is sometimes the most difficult time since other persons probably assume you are no longer bothered by it. You may even feel confused about what your real feelings were then and are now. Sometimes it helps to discuss these with someone else who can allow you to explore all that is going on. I wonder if you might like to talk about how things are going now."

Allowing a year for the postdivorce adjustment permits the individual to go through the cycle of important annual markers, such as the birthday of the ex-spouse, the wedding date, the birthdays of children, holidays, and other times which typically carry a considerable emotional load for an individual. The first time each of these dates occurs, the individual is likely to engage in a process of remembering what it was like on this day a few years ago and thus to some extent disengage himself emotionally from the former situation.

We have now examined in detail the sequence of processes from the first consideration of divorce through the postdivorce period. In most individuals, this process will cover approximately two to four years. One or several crisis points will occur during this lengthy span of change. At each of these points the pastor-counselor has specific tasks as part of the counseling process.

The Divorce Crises

The six stages outlined here could be condensed into fewer or expanded into more, since they are merely guideposts along the road of becoming disengaged from another with whom one has been extensively involved in many complex and pervasive ways. In this process there are at least three major crises:

(1) The crisis relating to the process of making a decision about divorce (stages one, two, and sometimes three above). This is a crisis because it usually involves a radical shift in one's self-concept, probably major changes in living arrangements, and one's acceptability with most of the significant persons in his life. For example, one young man was very upset about his

divorce because he was the only person in his family whose marriage had ended in this way. As a result of this event, he was deeply disturbed, the root cause being the shattering of his own self-concept and the feeling of having disgraced the family.

(2) The crisis of the divorce process itself (stages four and five above). If the feelings between the divorcing spouses are mutually cordial, and if no legal contest occurs, this crisis may be the least difficult of the three. On the other hand, if the spouses engage in the legal charges and countercharges of a contested divorce, this crisis may assume major proportions and may then generate other secondary crises that involve loss of self-esteem, anxiety, and possibly threats of physical harm. In this situation, the pastor will at times be supportive, at other times he will help the individuals to consider the effects of the battle on all parties concerned, and at other times seek to place the current conflict in the longer time perspective of adjustment to the changes which are occurring.

(3) The crisis of postdivorce adjustment (stage six, although this may begin in stage four above). This includes the readjustment to physical separation, moving personal items and clothes (and perhaps furniture) out of what one thought of as "home," changes in daily routines, sometimes much idle time, and other aspects of readjustment to living either alone or with relatives or friends. This also may precipitate other secondary crises, such as failure of one of the ex-spouses to keep promises made as part of the divorce agreement, re-entry into dating or other singles' activities, relationships with friends who are still married, family pressures, financial needs, care of children, and other potential problems.

233

THE MINISTER'S ROLE
IN THE CRISES OF DIVORCE

Although we have traced the process of divorce, it is important to emphasize the pastor's role in these crises. Although objective events may appear to be similar when the pastor compares two or more couples, the focus in divorce counseling is upon the meaning of these events for the individuals concerned. Crises in the divorce process occur when the individuals interpret the events as overwhelming and beyond their control in some way. The pastor's task is to assist the individuals to distinguish clearly among the confused meanings and to organize their personal resources to respond constructively to the divorce situation.

The pastor's role as counselor in this situation is to permit the individual to discover the meanings of divorce for him. Is divorce forbidden among his relatives, or is it perhaps almost expected? Does the divorce trigger earlier feelings of rejection or alienation by one's parents? Is the divorce an ineffective effort to return to adolescence or possibly childhood? Does the individual feel that God and/or the church will reject him because of divorce? These and related feelings of failure and rejection may be a central theme in the divorce crisis.

The pastor must be prepared to let the individual examine his feelings of being in a double-bind situation in the divorce. Since at deep levels the individual has sought acceptance in marriage, perhaps even fleeing from other friendships except the marriage, the counselee may feel that he cannot please the mate but cannot live without the mate either. How realistic is this interpretation? Are there other sources for friend-

234

ships and support than the marriage? Is the pattern of the "damned if I do and damned if I don't" related only to the marital partner or generalized to other situations as well? Does it have its roots in the individual's childhood? Depending upon the minister's training, he may provide limited counseling in these areas. When it becomes obvious that the divorce is only one symptom of some type of personality inadequacy or conflict, then the minister may consider securing consultation for his counseling or referring the individual to another professional who is more qualified and has the time to work with a more generalized personality problem.

If the individual felt rejected by the mate in the divorce process, there will probably be a grief process similar to the process that occurs in the loss of a loved one by death (see stage six above). In this situation of feeling rejected, typical grief reactions may occur. These include:

a) Initial shock and disbelief that divorce could "happen to me." This may result in futile attempts to ignore, repress, or reject the message and reality of divorce.

b) A crisis situation follows in which the individual seeks frantically for help from any source in correcting the situation or in adjusting to the "news" of divorce.

c) A period of generalized passive acceptance may follow in which the reality and inevitability of divorce comes home to the individual. This may occur approximately two to six months after the initial announcement by the mate of an intention to divorce. This may also be accompanied by the individual's having depression, hostility, and/or counteraggressive moves toward the "offending, rejecting" spouse.

d) A period of readjustment during which the individual is able to reorganize his ego-resources to cope more constructively with the divorce and the resulting changes in life-style related to it. This readjustment may include neurotic defenses as well as coping mechanisms. Its success will depend heavily on whether the individual develops healthy coping processes.

The minister's role in this process depends on the point at which he first comes in contact with the individual. If at reaction *a*, the minister will need to provide stable support to let the person know there are others who will stand with him in receiving the shock of the mate's desire for a divorce. Allowing the counselee to repeat the unbelievability of the divorce request will help the person to accept the reality of the situation.

If the minister enters the scene at *b*, he may represent one of the resources to which the individual can turn in the crisis. The minister may also need to remind the individual of genuine personal resources and strengths which the counselee actually does have with which to confront the divorce crisis. In addition, the minister may assist the individual to secure legal or other resources which may be necessary in the divorce proceedings.

In *c* and *d* the situation is often such that no genuine reconciliation efforts are possible. If the other spouse refuses to participate in counseling or other adjustment efforts, or if other conditions make divorce the only constructive solution to an intolerable situation, the minister may need to help the individual understand how the church or other important groups consider divorce. From the church's perspective, divorce is not a reason for excluding the person, but rather an admission that the marriage has not been successful, and its termination seems to be the least harmful solution. At every point the minister must convey to the person that he, by God's grace, continues to be just as acceptable now as formerly and that there are possibilities for new life which can come out of the ashes of a destroyed marriage.

In contrast, the individual who feels relief and satisfaction as a result of his divorce will also face psychological adjustments of a different type (see stage 6 above). Typically they occur in this sequence:

a) Initial relief at being away from what was perceived as an intolerable situation. This may express itself in a refusal to date others, an attitude that the mate never really understood "my" feelings, or perhaps a flight into many dating and other activities.

b) This may be followed by a growing attitude that it was primarily the mate's fault that the marriage did not succeed. The most serious consequence of this attitude may be that the individual becomes convinced that he was "right" and that there is no need for him to make any changes in his own style of living and personality.

c) If the person lacks insight into the dynamics of the divorce process, he may seek either a mate who is totally opposite from the first mate or a mate who interacts in the same manner as did the first mate.

The minister's task in counseling with this second type of reaction to divorce is again to enable the individual to separate fact from fantasy. Was the marriage situation actually a very painful experience? In what way? To what extent was the divorce precipitated by the individual who now considers everything to have been the ex-spouse's fault? To what extent does the counselee have insight into the real reasons for divorce? Is the individual able to benefit from these insights and make actual changes in his behavior which will improve the chances for relating more constructively with another person? Does the individual have any plans for remarriage? If within a year of the divorce, is it probable that the remarriage is in part a reaction to feeling unhappy in being divorced, rather than a genuinely healthy acceptance of the new mate by the divorced individual? These are issues which the individual needs to consider. The pastor, of course, will not present them in the question form outlined here, but he must be aware of them and allow, even at times encourage, the counselee to face these issues.

Some divorced persons may experience a variety of guilt reactions to the divorce. These may be expressed as "if only I had done differently . . ." or "it was all my fault." There is also the problem of aligning the divorce situation with one's original marriage vow "till death us do part." This vow is a statement of the *intention* of the individuals at the time they enter marriage. In the face of divorce, one must now decide whether his original intention was well founded and whether in some way one has gone back on his promise. At deeper levels, it may be a way of asking whether one is still acceptable to family, friends, and others. Both psychologically and religiously, guilt must be resolved through forgiveness and a renewed acceptance of the individual by significant persons in his life.

Where guilt reactions occur, the minister can be a channel of forgiveness and renewal through the counseling process. He may also assist the individual to become involved in appropriate group relationships that will confirm his acceptability as a divorced person. At

deeper levels, the minister may discuss theological issues of guilt and God's forgiveness with the individual.
This is appropriate as part of the broader counseling
process, although the pastor must be careful that this
intellectual discussion is not used as a way of avoiding
examination of painful emotional feelings.

Divorce is often related to a change in status in the
life of one or both spouses. Many divorces begin in the
first year of marriage because this is a period of rapid
adjustment to the major change from single to married
life. Other critical periods are the arrival of the first
child (thus allowing a two-against-one situation),
spouse's graduation from university or other education
program, establishing oneself in a job or business or
profession, a change to different duties in one's job,
major financial adjustments or reversals, anticipation of
middle age, death of close relatives or friends, circum-
stantial opportunities for becoming involved in an extra-
marital affair, and major changes in the behavior of family or friends. None of these is actually the basic reason
for divorce, but in each situation underlying inadequate
adjustments may be exposed by the added stress of a
crisis in the life of one or both mates, thus leading to
the additional crises of divorce.

In counseling with an individual for whom a major
life change has precipitated consideration of divorce,
the central task is clarification of the sources of stress
and the identification of the threat involved. Once this
occurs, the counselee can be assisted to find more constructive ways for handling the original crisis. In addition, one spouse may be helped to discover how he can
give essential support, comfort, and care to the other
under stress. If this does not occur, then the counselee
needs the aid of the pastor in making realistic plans to

239

resolve each crisis, first the precipitating event and then the divorce.

Divorce is usually a more or less permanent separation. Although it is possible that former spouses who are divorced from each other can sometimes shift into a stable acquaintance or friendship pattern, it is very unlikely that this will occur. The circumstances of divorce usually can be handled much more simply and adequately if the parties involved consider the divorce to be a permanent and absolute severance of any relation whatsoever. It is not too extreme to suggest that divorce should be as complete and permanent as the death of a spouse. However, practical problems of child support or property may force ex-mates to continue contact with each other on a friendship basis for the sake of their children or in order to maintain child support or alimony payments. If a couple decides to terminate the marriage, then it should be a clean and complete break.

In the planning and anticipation of the postdivorce adjustment, the pastor has the opportunity to assist the individuals to clarify any lingering hope or dependency needs in relation to the ex-spouse. If an individual hopes to continue on a friendly basis with the former mate, the pastor should gently confront the individual with the meaning of these relationships. Is continuing to see the ex-mate a result of guilt about the divorce, a way of "fixing" or undoing an undesirable divorce? Is it a diffused hostility toward the other partner which is expressed in subtle comments, depreciating comparisons, or flaunting of the individual's "better" life now that the divorce is over? Is it related to dependency and anxiety about being left alone or being unable to succeed in any new relationships with the opposite sex? Is it a way of continuing to use the ex-mate as a babysitter for the children under the guise of visitation rights? These and other subtle, often unrealized, motivations may underlie attempts to continue a relationship with the ex-mate after divorce.

In some postdivorce situations, the person may feel especially vulnerable emotionally and harbor a hidden fear that he will be left alone. This may cause the individual to avoid any further contacts with the opposite sex, to reject his own sexuality, or to be very defensive in relation to potential future mates. More severe psychological reactions may trigger a variety of acting-out behaviors which are calculated to secure attention while at the same time punishing the attender.

The pastor has an opportunity to assist the divorced person to feel accepted through the pastor's own contacts with the person as well as by enabling the individual to become involved in appropriate groups. The minister may also guide mature lay persons in the church or community to initiate friendships with divorced persons to let them know that they are still wanted and desirable as persons for whom God and the church cares. There is the possibility also that other persons who have successfully readjusted to their own divorces may be enlisted, under the minister's guidance, to maintain friendships with newly divorced persons. In this relation of empathetic sharing, the person adjusting to divorce may be able to receive support from others who have gone through similar experiences. He may also be able to talk more freely about personal feelings surrounding the divorce. In some churches, church school classes or other groups may be organized especially for single adults which typically include many divorced persons. Traditional couples' classes might be sensitized to the need to reach out to divorced persons in helping them feel accepted. Sometimes the minister may enlist the divorced person in volunteer activities in the church or community as part of the readjustment process.

Regardless of the circumstances of the divorce, each partner will need some postdivorce counseling. Some writers even suggest a formal ceremony of "uncoupling" or divorce, somewhat parallel to the wedding ceremony in its psychological function of having the community acknowledge and accept the new status of the divorced person. Since a divorced person is in considerably different psychological circumstances from one who has never married, the minister can be available through counseling to help the person find his way in this new life situation which is different in several respects from either single, married, or widowed life-styles.

As has been described in earlier chapters, the general format of crisis counseling by the minister is short-term contact with a person experiencing major acute life changes that tend to overwhelm his or her typical coping patterns. Since the process of divorce extends over a period of time—from at least one year to perhaps several years—it should not be inferred that this constitutes one long, almost chronic crisis (a contradiction in terms). Instead, there are at least three rather specific and separate crises that typically occur in this period. These were described above as the crisis of deciding about divorce, the potential crisis of the actual legal actions necessitated by the divorce decision, and the crisis of postdivorce adjustment. The concepts, procedures, and suggestions of this chapter must be understood as based upon the fundamental principles of crisis intervention and counseling as well as placed in the context of both the individual's life history and the family dynamics which he has experienced in both the childhood family and the adult marriage. With this interrelationship in mind, we will briefly consider five situations which are closely related to the crises of divorce: desertion, children of divorce, remarriage, multiple divorce, and annulment.

Desertion

Desertion has often been termed the poor person's divorce. Except for the legal aspects, desertion is very similar in its psychological dynamics to divorce. There is a period when the deserting mate first begins to consider this as a possible solution to an unhappy marriage. He may often not announce his impending absence from the mate, which then creates for the deserted mate an ambiguous situation in which that spouse does not know whether to expect the partner's return. As a result, the remaining spouse may be left with unpaid bills, children to support, perhaps little or no income, and other serious problems in addition to the basic crisis of shock, loss of self-esteem, and related psychological damage.

The pain and problems of desertion are often compounded because it is likely to happen to persons who in our society have less than average personal and psychological coping ability to meet a situation that is more difficult and ambiguous than a clear-cut divorce. The pastor of a deserted person will need first to be sure that basic necessities such as food, housing, and daily needs of that person, and usually children, are met.

Once the daily needs are stabilized, the pastor can

begin the counseling intervention described above under stages two, three, and four. In addition, there is
the important task of helping the remaining spouse to
clarify feelings of sudden rejection, loneliness, and anger and to work through these. In this process the minister may also enable the spouse to identify his or her own
behavior that may have helped to cause the desertion.
Efforts at reconciliation may also be appropriate. If the
deserting party can be located, the pastor may initiate
contacts to help that person work through his own
feelings about the remaining spouse as well as discover
more constructive ways of either rebuilding the marriage or making a clear divorce decision. If financial
expense is a problem, inexpensive legal clinics may be
located by the pastor for the parties as needed.

Children of Divorce

When children are involved in a divorce, the divorcing partners are usually very concerned with the impact
of the divorce upon them. There is the decision of
which mate (since it certainly is not necessarily the
mother) will have custody and daily responsibility for
the children, the extent and schedule of visits with the
other parent (if any), provision of child support, and
many practical matters. In addition, the divorcing mates
usually wonder what to tell the children about the divorce and how having only one parent present will affect
the children's development.

This also is a very broad topic which we can only
mention briefly. Each year approximately one percent
of the children under eighteen years of age in the
United States are involved in a divorce or annulment
procedure. Among children under age eighteen, ap-

proximately 10 percent of the white and 35 percent of the nonwhite groups are not living with both parents.[17] Parents Without Partners, a national organization of one-parent families, publishes a magazine, "The Single Parent." Perhaps the central task of the pastor is to enable the counselee parents to examine their own feelings about the children in relation to the divorce. Does the divorced person blame the children for the marriage breakdown? Is there an attempt to overcompensate for having only one parent in various subtle ways? Does the parent feel, perhaps without acknowledging it, that he really did want to eliminate the influence, and hence the threat, of the mate on the children's lives? Does the remaining mate feel adequate to the task of parenting?

The pastor may allow the parent to discuss, and possibly role-play, difficult situations relating to the divorce. For example, the child may ask, "Why don't you and (daddy/mommy) live together so we can all be happy?" The parent must be helped to be both supportive and honest in the answers to this and similar questions. In response to this question, the parent might answer, "I love you and will continue to be with you, and (daddy/mommy) loves you also. We just could not seem to work together, somewhat like you and (name of a child) sometimes have difficulty playing. We felt we could all be happier as we are now than if we had stayed together and fussed with each other all the time." It is important that the answer convey to the child that the parents are still clearly and definitely dependable and available (according to the circumstances of the divorce), that the child is sin-

[17] Abbott Ferriss, *Indicators of Change in the American Family*, (New York: Russell Sage Foundation, 1970), p. 71.

cerely loved, and that as much as possible the child will have a normal childhood.

At a deeper level, the child really has, in a sense, "four parents." These are, of course, the father and the mother, and in addition, the mother as presented and described by the father and the father as presented and described by the mother. Even if one parent is now gone, the child continues to have both the remaining parent and the "other parent which this parent interprets to the child." What, then, are the feelings of the remaining parent about the divorced spouse? What can he or she reply to the child and still be honest? The pastor can provide for the divorced parent an opportunity to consider these deeper feelings, their impact on the children, and specific ways in which to convey the most constructive interpretations of the situation. In this way the pastor can assist the individual to avoid or resolve the crisis of relating to the children as a divorced parent who is in some way responsible for the children's being to some extent deprived of the other parent.

The pastor needs to be alert to the possible crises which the children in a divorce situation may experience directly. There are a variety of ways in which children may express their feelings of crisis, depending heavily upon their ages. Preschool children may experience restlessness, bad dreams, intensified fears of being left alone in church school, day nursery, or other situations, and related changes of mood. Older children may demonstrate crisis feelings by failing to do as well as formerly in school, moodiness, enuresis (bed-wetting), fingernail-biting, bursts of inappropriate anger, and noncooperativeness. Adolescents may be overtly rebellious or aggressive, withdraw from former friends or activities, use alcohol or other drugs, or become overly involved in romantic affairs. These and other behaviors are ways in which the child of the divorced parents is usually communicating his anxiety, anger, and shock.

When the pastor notes unusual behavior changes in children and adolescents in a divorce situation, he may take the initiative in discussing these changes with the parent in counseling or pastoral care contacts. The pastor may initiate counseling directly with older children and adolescents. Sometimes a family counseling situation may develop. In other situations, the pastor may need to suggest referral to an appropriate professional person such as a psychologist or psychiatrist. Usually the pastor can discuss with one or both parents the possibility of a crisis impact on the children so that they can also be alert for these signs of excessive stress. Helpful references concerning children of divorce are Steinzor and Despert.[18]

Remarriage

Most divorced persons eventually remarry, and several good references are available in this area.[19] If the remarriage of a divorced person occurs after that period of time which will allow for adequate readjustment and recovery from the divorce (usually a year or more), then the pastor will utilize the basic premarital counseling approaches.[20] The major changes involve the careful

[18] Bernard Steinzor, *When Parents Divorce: A New Approach to New Relationships* (New York: Pantheon Books, 1969); Juliette L. Despert, *Children of Divorce* (Garden City, N. Y.: Doubleday & Co., 1953).

[19] Jessie Bernard, *Remarriage: A Study of Marriage* (New York: Holt, Rinehart and Winston, 1956).

[20] Aaron L. Rutledge, *Pre-Marital Counseling* (Cambridge, Mass.: Schenkman Publishing Co., 1966); Stewart, *The Minister as Marriage Counselor*.

consideration by the two potential mates of their feelings about the previous marriage. How will the anticipated marriage be different from previous unsuccessful ones? What was learned in the previous marriage that will now enable this one to be happier and more successful?

Other areas which will probably be modified in premarital counseling with divorced persons include a discussion of relationships of the new parent to the former parent who may still be visiting children, and the combining of two families, if both partners have children from previous marriage. If one partner has children but the other does not, then this childless partner will have to adjust to a ready-made family in which children may have ties with the absent original parent. Matters of living arrangements are also involved, since the new mate may be "invading" the home of the children and be seen by them as an interloper. These situations offer potential crisis times as remarriage is approached. The pastor can help to defuse these if he uses the premarital counseling sessions to allow consideration of these problems which are unique to the remarriage situation.

Multiple Divorce

In some instances the pastor may be confronted with individuals who are terminating a second unsatisfactory marriage, or even a third or fourth. The basic divorce process and divorce crises are still likely to be present. In addition, however, there is the possibility that a second divorce may indicate more severe personality maladjustments that prevent the individual from living intimately with another person for an extended period of time. If the pastor suspects this, a referral to a psy-

chologist or psychiatrist at some appropriate point for
a personality assessment may be important to clarify
whether crisis counseling approaches by the pastor are
the most appropriate basic therapy. This does not
diminish the need for pastoral care of these persons,
since they continue to face the crises of divorce, sometimes in greater severity. The person's greater sense of
failure and inadequacy may be expressed in statements
such as, "Anybody can make a mistake once, but if
twice or more, there must be something seriously wrong
with me." With a second divorce, the chance of a successful third marriage drops to less than 40 percent.[21]
With multiple-divorced persons, the additional task of
the pastor is to determine clearly how much of the
troubled behavior of the person is crisis and how much
is due to long-standing, inadequate personality and
coping processes.

Annulment

The process of annulment is similar to the divorce
process, since in many cases annulment is only a technical legal term for divorce. The three basic stages of
decision, legal proceedings, and postannulment adjustment crises are very likely to be present in the person
who is terminating marriage in this manner. In addition,
since annulment is likely to involve younger (often teen-
aged) mates, the pastor may need to deal with an additional crisis involving one or both mates and one or
both sets of their parents or other relatives. Annulment
may also indicate a marriage that was hasty, ill-consid-
ered, or in reaction to parental pressures; and thus it

[21] Landis, *Making the Most of Marriage.*

is likely that the pastor will have the further task of assisting reconciliation or adjustments between parents and the child whose marriage is annulled. Here principles of family dynamics and counseling are central in addition to crisis intervention skills.

SUMMARY

In applying the principles of crisis intervention to the divorce process, the pastor's basic step is to clarify his own understanding of divorce in our society as a legal procedure, from a theological and philosophical perspective, and in his own personal experience. The three basic crisis situations of divorce (decision about divorce, legal procedures relative to actual divorce decree, and postdivorce adjustment) are high-visibility points of the total divorce process which may extend over a period of at least one or two years, usually three or four years, and in some cases a much longer span of time. As an aid to the details of this process and the pastor's opportunities for ministry, six rather specific stages of this total sequence have been described. The minister may wish to reorganize these, keeping in mind that they actually may overlap, merge, or occasionally be skipped in a specific divorce situation. The minister's practical functioning in regard to the crises of divorce and in five divorce-related situations, which may also generate crises in an individual or family, has also been considered.

Chapter IX

THE MINISTER, THE CONGREGATION, AND COMMUNITY CRISIS SERVICES

This book has pointed to some of the aspects of the total context of operation, the tradition, and expected functions of the clergyman that show him to be uniquely suited for the role of crisis counselor, a role in which he already spends a large amount of his time. In order to assist him in developing his effectiveness in this task and opportunity to a higher level of competence, details of crisis theory, the crisis counseling process, and some specific forms of intervention have been presented. Elaboration of both the nature of crisis and the way in which the minister may function effectively in its resolution were illustrated by what remains something of a prototype of crisis, and the one with which many ministers must engage themselves with more frequency than others, the grief situation. Finally, because of the centrality of the family and its constellation of relationships in producing human beings as they are, because a majority of people still live in the context of some form of family when they experience their crises, because family crisis itself is rather common, and again because of the frequency with which the minister encounters crisis in a family setting, a description of family systems on different levels of functioning and also the crises of divorce were examined as necessary parts of the minister's total understanding of crisis and his more enlightened and effective helping.

It now remains to consider the larger context of the minister's arena of functioning with regard to the nature of the congregation and the minister's relationship to other crisis agencies and mental health professionals. This last chapter will seek to sketch that picture briefly.

THE MINISTER AND COMMUNITY CRISIS SERVICES

The minister is called and ordained not only to serve his own congregation directly, but the larger community within and for which the congregation exists. He ordinarily performs this service through direct helpful contact with persons and families, in a variety of educational activities, and through a number of functions within other established helping agencies.

Fulfilling His Traditional Role

The emphasis of this book has been clearly on the minister's own work, operating within his own congregation as a crisis counselor—one of the functions which both he and his congregation expect him to perform. This does not mean, of course, that the only persons he sees are members of his congregation, but it is the institution within and out of which he does his work. The point has been made that by fulfilling this role conscientiously he is not only being faithful to the ministry of the church but is also to be viewed as a very important frontline mental health professional. In several places his unique advantages over other mental health professionals have been mentioned, presuming that he capitalizes upon these advantages and does so with competence. An excellent presentation elaborating this point has been made, happily enough, by a non-ministerial professional in the field of community psychiatry. In summary she states that the clergyman has a population focus (the congregation and its constituency), is known by his population and knows them, is less threatening for many people to approach than a psychiatrist or anyone else in a psychiatric clinic, is likely to see people at an early stage of disturbance or in crisis, may respond within a short period of time to a distress call, and, because of his knowledge of a person, may assess the situation or condition more rapidly, does not expect a fee, has the initiative to intervene, is expected to call in homes, remains close to those whom he has counseled through other forms of relationship, offers a variety of modes for continuing care, has a position of authority that may be sensitively utilized in some instances, is in a context in which guilt may be effectively dealt with, and has ritualistic structures which are helpful to many people.[1]

When the clergyman does persistently and well what is given by his situation as a minister, he is making a significant contribution to persons and to the mental health of the community.

Working with Community Crisis Services

However, the minister also has additional opportunities by relating himself to mental health agencies

---

[1] Caplan, *Helping the Helpers*, pp. 16-36.

in general and crisis intervention and suicide prevention centers in particular. Many ministers should associate themselves to these agencies in forms specific to the
minister's own interests and abilities and the needs of
those organizations. This directive, while important,
should not be misunderstood. Although the minister
who has no concern whatsoever for the effectiveness of
the operation of mental health services in his community should examine the quality of his own caring for
persons, it is not being suggested that every minister
could or should actually work in some way with these
agencies, or that they are the only, or even the most
important, community services that he should support
with his money, time, and talent. The major point of
this exhortation is merely to declare that each one of
us exists in the midst of many distressed and disturbed
persons. There are a variety of ways in which these
needs might be met. A number of different types of
agencies or programs should be in any community in
order to serve these persons. Among these are crisis
intervention and suicide prevention centers. These
should be operating in every community of any size,
either as separate agencies or as an important and available function of a broader agency or institution, such
as a general mental health clinic, public health clinic,
hospital, Council of Churches counseling center. Many
ministers have this type of service to persons as one of
their high priorities and also have the training and experience to be useful to such a program. Such ministers should actively search out these opportunities.

One study clarifies the great gap between the stated
care and actual behavior of ministers in this regard. A
survey was taken of a hundred ministers in order to get
a picture of their mental health activities as defined

by prevention, counseling, and referral. Only two felt that they were forced against their own desires into such a role. On the other hand, ninety-eight expressed great interest and concern for this aspect of the minister's work and felt that they should be involved. Yet, even though a majority carried on counseling and other preventive activities within the church, only seven belonged to any type of mental health organization,[2] and it might be presumed that some of these even were not direct service agencies. Recognizing the tremendous demands on the minister's time and the existence of other high priorities, this picture remains a bleak commentary on what we claim our concern to be.

One word of warning: The response by other mental health professionals and even lay persons will not always be an enthusiastic welcome to the minister who volunteers himself. However, this realism should not deter the clergy from proposing the word that he is a legitimate and important professional in this field, especially that of crisis, and that he is available. He will often, if not always, find a place of significant opportunity for helping.

Ministers are, in fact, working with satisfaction to themselves, with value to agencies, and with both direct and indirect advantages to persons in need in a number of different capacities. A clergyman may carry to board membership his knowledge of effective organizational behavior, personal relationships, program supervision, or finances. As a member of a personnel committee he may use his own congregation and organize other ministers to use theirs as a resource for the selection of a

[2] W. Kenneth Bentz, "Consensus Between Role Expectations and Role Behavior among Ministers," *Community Mental Health Journal,* IV (August, 1968), 301-6.

high quality of volunteer worker. If he happens to be one with clinical skills, he may be on a clinical services committee, do face-to-face or telephone counseling, serve as one who makes emergency visits to persons who in their distress have called a telephone crisis center, or even become a trainer of lay volunteers.

Since there has been an explosive increase in the number of such telephone crisis services within the last few years, the church itself being the initiator and sponsor of many of them, and with many of the others looking to ministers for different forms of support, it might be appropriate to comment upon the pastor's role in and responsibility to them, along with some dangers of which to be aware.

The point has already been made that such a form of helping persons is an appropriate place for ministers to invest themselves, and some of the ways in which they might do so have already been listed. In some communities, individual ministers or groups of them have initiated discussions that have led to the development of telephone services. In these instances, one would assume that they have consulted from the very beginning with mental health professionals in their area for several reasons. The most important one is, of course, to profit from their insights in the surveying of community needs, the planning for the selection, training, and supervision of the workers, and the implementation of day-to-day operational guidelines and procedures. This is not to suggest that everything that every mental health professional says should be accepted as final law. That becomes quite clear as we observe their differing among themselves as to whether the community needs such a service, whether it can accomplish the purposes proposed, whether lay people can do such work, how much training is necessary before work on the telephone begins, and other issues. Nevertheless, such input is important in making those decisions necessary for getting an agency underway. Second, the professionals in a community should always be kept fully informed of what is taking place, even if some of them are in disagreement with the whole or parts of the project. A professional's suspicions concerning the operation may often be more damaging to its usefulness in the community than his knowledge of its actual weaknesses. Third, some of these professionals should be involved in some way in the ongoing program through board membership and policy-making, training, supervision, and consultation. Most of those telephone agencies that have sought, with whatever good intentions, to offer their services to a community without having these forms of relationship with mental health professionals have had significant barriers to overcome, have often done as much harm as they have good, and occasionally have failed to overcome the barriers and have passed out of existence.

It has not only been the case that some of the telephone services through a lack of wisdom have failed to have adequate professional consultation and supervision, but others have actually had an antiprofessional tone about them. The assumption of some of these, particularly those that are youth-oriented, is that any young person can automatically communicate well with any other young person, that any former drug-user by virtue of that fact can help a drug-user, and that merely openness, acceptance, and unstructured relationships are therapeutic. These assumptions are not substantiated by the actual data. As a matter of fact, there

257

may be considerable harm done.[3] Ministers should associate themselves with such unsupervised activities and such unchallenged assumptions only with the greatest caution, and only then in consultation with a mental health professional personally and with the view to seeking to bring some upgrading of the service through the introduction of professional supervision. While volunteers in such services may very well be young people, former drug-users, members of the counterculture, or whatever, they still must be selected on the basis of their therapeutic potential for those in distress, must be trained, and must have professional supervision.

Community Crisis

One area in which most ministers have very little training, and only by coincidence any experience, is that of community-wide crisis, such as a geographical area might suffer as a result of earthquakes, tornadoes, hurricanes, or floods, or in community crisis reactive to significant and sudden loss of a number of lives of persons through an explosion or fire or other accident. As a result of students' creative response to an earthquake in February 1971, the School of Theology at Claremont has offered a course that has had as its objective the training of theological students in the handling of both physical and psychological needs of a population during and immediately following a disaster, but this type of training is rare. Noteworthy is the fact that students themselves organize and operate the course.

[3] Paul Torop and Karen Torop, "Hot Lines and Youth Culture Values," *American Journal of Psychiatry*, CXXIX (December, 1972), 730-33.

Minister, Congregation, and Community

The minister, along with other community helpers (doctors, nurses, social workers, schoolteachers), is in a unique position to work to alleviate overwhelming community needs. A newspaper feature has reported the service of the Center for Preventive Psychiatry in White Plains, New York, in the aftermath of the flood suffered in the city of Corning following Hurricane Agnes.[4] The mental health team identified as the basic psychological needs of the people those to express fully their feelings about their losses of homes, possessions, family, friends, and their feelings of helplessness, anxiety, despair, anger. The people in the community who did not have such direct losses often were troubled by guilt over having escaped, an irrational, but nonetheless real and troublesome, feeling.

The primary methodology of the mental health team was to get people to share their feelings with one another in groups, utilizing as far as possible the natural and already organized groups that exist in any community: professional societies, civic and service clubs. A second methodology of the team was to meet with the teachers and school administrators in order to help them work effectively with the types of problems they would have to deal with when the children returned to school, enabling these natural community leaders to assist those for whom they are responsible in expressing their feelings and in dealing with the realities of the situation without denial. A third means of meeting the psychological emergencies of the area was to set up a twenty-four-hour "help and rumor" line, alleviating people's anxieties both by crisis counseling and by simply giving accurate information.

[4] " 'Crisis' Therapy Tried in Corning," *New York Times*, October 29, 1972, p. 65.

Following the disaster and during the whole emergency period, only a very few suicides and psychotic breaks were recorded in Corning, in contrast with another city which had suffered equally from the flood but where no similar intensive mental health services were rendered and where the rate of suicide and psychotic reactions doubled. This has been interpreted as one bit of evidence of the value of the procedures. It requires no imagination to see where a minister would fit into such a situation, with his already established community leadership, his relatively open door to civic and service clubs, the meaningful symbols of the church and the faith, the congregation and its smaller units, his visiting of families and groups of families, and his participation on newly organized emergency mental health teams.

The Minister's Relationship
with Other Mental Health Professionals

The way in which this section heading is phrased assumes what has already been made clear to the reader of this book, that by virtue of being an effective and faithful minister of the church, the minister is in fact an important mental health professional with a unique contribution to make. However, it should not be misinterpreted as suggesting that all or even most psychiatrists, psychologists, and psychiatric social workers and nurses accept this assumption as self-evident. To the contrary, some have had the type of early personal experiences or contacts with ministers or with their own clients that cause them either to be dubious about the value of the minister's work with persons or to be downright negative about it. Others have not even had the awareness to consider the possible values of a close working relationship with the clergy.

Some of the psychotherapeutic professionals' suspicions concerning ministers are founded in experience more substantial than their own ignorance and prejudice, although these may also be present. There are ministers who are naïve psychologically, ineffective as pastors and counselors, and who hold and communicate attitudes and utilize methods of handling emotions and drives that may be harmful to some persons. Certainly we all realize that the qualifications for being a minister are much more varied than those for other professions, and therefore to use the label of minister says absolutely nothing about educational and other training prerequisites, in contrast with the medical, psychological, and to a somewhat lesser degree, the social work professionals.

Nevertheless, an increasing number of ministers are better trained in dealing with persons and their problems, and many others who are not formally trained are sensitive and competent and helpful human beings within the framework of their vocation as ministers. These persons form a great pool of helping resources for a large percentage of our population, and their lives and ministry do in fact touch more persons in some ways than does the service of other professionals. At the same time, since the training of ministers is so varied, when they get into the area of assisting persons in crisis, there is still much to learn from the knowledge and skills of other professionals.

The following diagram shows some of the lines for interprofessional support and collaboration in a full therapeutic program for meeting the needs of individuals and families in crisis.

Psychotherapeutic Professionals   *Ministers*

1. Teacher (of Crisis Theory and Methodology) ⟶ Learner

2. Consultant ⟶ Primary Crisis Counselor

3. Primary Crisis Counselor

   ⟶ First Crisis Contact

   ⟶ Supportive Pastoral Care

   ⟶ Postcrisis Follow-up

4. Community Mental Health Programs (Education and Service) ⟶ Educational and Service Functions

5. Member of Crisis Intervention Team ⟷ Member of Crisis Intervention Team

First, the teacher-learner relationship presumes what is usually true, that the professional psychotherapist has accumulated a certain body of knowledge of personality development, psychodynamics, psychopathology, and interpersonal relationships and has developed certain insights and skills related to therapeutic communication that the majority of ministers have not had the opportunity to obtain, even though we may have considerable experience in dealing with persons. Since ministers are so strategically located throughout most communities and by virtue of their position are related to such a large number of people and are so easily and readily available to additional numbers, it only makes good sense for the mental health professionals of every community to offer and the ministers of every community to seek specialized continuing education in the area of understanding individual and family dynamics and improving counseling skills.

Second, simply in performing his usual expected work, ministers will frequently be the primary crisis counselor to many persons and families (in grief, loss of job, change of place of living, family conflict, divorce). In many instances he will be able to assist persons through these crises successfully, anxiety will diminish, mood will lift, decisions will be made, constructive action initiated. He will do this through the meaning of his position (his symbol power), the strength of his genuine humanity, and whatever knowledge he has of crisis counseling. On occasion, the nature of the person or family undergoing crisis or the intensity of the crisis itself, combined with the minister's perception of his own lack of clarity concerning the issues involved, the interventions to utilize, and possible directions to take, may lead the minister to seek one or more consultation sessions with another professional. This is a case in which the minister would get an appointment with the other professional, describe the total situation, discuss all the issues, and receive guidance from the professional as to procedures in continuing to work with the person in crisis. The minister continues to be the primary counselor, with assistance from the psychotherapist.

There may be several sources and forms of this arrangement. Some ministers may be fortunate enough to have one or more such professionals in their own congregations who would be willing to provide this type of consultation occasionally to their own pastor without charge and as a part of their own lay ministry. Or some professional might be found outside of the congregation who for other reasons might donate some amount of time. Most ministers, however, will probably not be this fortunate.

Three other routes remain open. If the mental health professional is in private practice or working for a private institution or agency, it is proper for that person to expect a fee for his consultation services. Either the minister himself would need to pay this, or hopefully the congregation could see the value of such a procedure and put this item in its budget. Only a couple of hundred dollars would purchase time quite adequate for most minister's needs over the period of a year.

A second route is described by Ruth Caplan, the purchase of regular group consultation services for its ministers by the denominational budget of a geographical area.[5] Most denominational or faith groups have such administrative budgets, as well as the contacts

[5] *Helping the Helpers.*

necessary to employ competent professionals, neither of which most pastors of most small churches have.

A third route is available in those cities which have an organized Mental Health–Mental Retardation program, where, in order to receive federal funds, the agency is required to provide consultation for the various helping persons of its area.

The third form of interprofessional relationship in the crisis situation occurs when the minister is confronted with a situation in which he soon recognizes that the family is a deeply disturbed one, with strong and rigid dysfunctional communication and behavior patterns, or that the individual in crisis has elements of psychopathology that render a particular minister's usual crisis counseling procedures ineffective. In this case the minister would move toward referral or transferral to a psychiatrist or psychologist or other appropriate professional with the latter becoming the primary therapist. However, it should be clear that more often than not the minister stays in the picture. He remains the pastor to the person or persons involved through appropriate phone calls and visits, maintaining personal interest, representing the congregation and the faith, and supporting commitment to counseling. He may, in mutual understanding with the primary therapist, be in a situation to make emergency personal calls when the therapist or the person in crisis feels that this is important. Finally, when formal counseling is completed, the other professional might be very happy to know that the minister will provide follow-up pastoral care.

In the area of community mental health programs, there are a number of functions that the trained and sensitive minister might perform that would be in support of the efforts of the psychotherapeutic professions.

Some of these have already been mentioned in the discussion of the various roles of ministers in telephone crisis agencies. In addition to these, the dialogue established between the various professions may give the minister the opportunity to clarify to others the particular view of human life that the community of faith understands, reemphasizing for all persons in the helping professions the ultimate value of persons, the role of faith in individual's lives, the relationship of responsible (ethical) behavior to human well-being, and dimensions of being fully human that are not related only to materialistic pursuits. The frequent injection of this emphasis into interprofessional discussions and training programs, while not designed as a sneaky form of evangelism, should certainly have some effect of sensitizing mental health workers to how significant the religious perspective toward life might be to many of their own clients. This may then, occasionally, lead to other professionals' consulting with a minister whom they respect in regard to moral and religious dimensions of their clients' lives, or even making a referral to him.

Finally, in some places crisis intervention teams have been developed. The standard personnel are psychiatrists, psychologists, psychiatric social workers and nurses. In the light of possible working relationships mentioned in numbers 3 and 4 above, it would be logical for specially trained ministers to be members of such teams, for the mutual edification of all the professionals and in service of the persons in crisis.

THE CONGREGATION AS A CONTEXT FOR CRISIS MINISTRY

The minister must keep two things in mind at the same time as far as the acting out of his vocation is concerned. First, he does not exist only for his own congregation. Rather, as a part of and servant to and representative of the congregation, like the congregation, he exists for the world. Though "Christ loved the *church* and gave himself up for her" (Eph. 5:25), also "God so loved the *world* that he gave his only Son" (John 3:16). The church as the Body of Christ exists in the world for the same reason that Jesus himself did, to be God's Servant to all persons, to all humankind. This is our mandate to be involved in the larger community in whatever forms of service are appropriate to our interests, abilities, training, and the needs that are apparent to us. This should bring many ministers into professional interaction with the mental health sector. Second, at the same time that we participate in other agencies, alongside of other professionals, learning from them and working with them to meet human need, we must never lose sight of who we are and whose we are. We are a part of God's people, rendering our service out of commitment to him. Wherever we are, the congregation always forms the context for our activity. To say this is not only to speak of a particular mind-set with which we operate at all times, but much more concretely, it is a reminder of the specific values to persons and families in crisis of the community of faith in its organized life together.

Faith and Its Ritualistic Celebration

Every person lives by some internal impetus which might be properly called faith. It is that to which we commit ourselves as having some ultimacy, some overarching guiding significance for our lives. Individuals are not always fully aware of what this is for them, or, if somewhat aware, do not clearly and fully articulate it, and often do not celebrate it either alone or with other persons who share a similar faith. But faith has a potency, provides motivation, suggests goals and behavioral guidelines, *is* in a sense why a person is living and why he is living as he is at a given time.

The Judaeo-Christian faiths combine in a unique way for many people the dimensions of the long past, a tradition, including their own individual briefer pasts, the high significance of the present moment, and a serious emphasis on the future that is in some way linked with God's own future and is thereby secured by him and his love. Faith leads a person into an experience of his own ultimate worth, since he is one whom God loves ultimately and without condition. It suggests that the present should always be viewed in the light of God's activity on our behalf both in the past and in the future, no matter how unaware we may be of his caring at the moment. Thus, there is always meaning in the present, even though we do not *know* in the present precisely what it is, and there is hope for the future. This hope is not knowledge of the form of our future life and its meaning, but an assurance that, without taking responsible decision and action out of our hands, the future belongs to the God who does love us and act for us, and all this without a denial of the reality of what is *now* taking place.

The implications of this faith for a person in crisis as it has been defined in this book are obvious. The person in crisis is one who has begun to lose perspective, feels anxious and helpless, often depressed and worthless, frequently without hope, whose future seems to be blocked out, who even has lost sight of some of his own past. Faith as briefly outlined above is a direct counter-force to the dynamics of crisis.

This should not be misinterpreted to mean that the needs of a person in crisis will be met by the mere mouthings of doctrines, religious catch phrases, or the quick and casual quoting of scripture, although for some people appropriate verbalizations reflecting the realities of the experience of faith may be stabilizing. More effective is the ministry of the representative of the congregation, the pastor, with his symbol power communicating the faith, and being surrounded by the community of faith, joining with it in the group celebration of their common life, hearing and participating with this group in prayer, Scripture-reading, acts of praise in the midst of present suffering, hearing the Word proclaimed, all reemphasizing for the person who he is, who his support is (both the Lord and the congregation), and what his future may be. In addition, there are the smaller groups within the congregation, the classes, the study groups, men's, women's, or youth organizations, and those individuals who express their care and concern in a variety of ways. Emotions may be expressed, perspective broadened, the future opened, direct present support given, all in the service of crisis resolution.

Ruth Caplan has spoken of "the role of regular religious observance in preserving mental health." [6] She speaks of the provision of a certain order in an individual's life which is of continuing therapeutic value.

The fact that such observances are repeated at regular intervals steadily reinforces the message of discipline, structure, and identity. It regularly renews community contacts

[6] *Ibid.*, p. 35.

and devotion to that group's ideals by repeated exposure to signs of fellowship. As behavioral scientists have discovered, people need a *constant* flow of physical and social supplies and stimulation to maintain their well-being.[7]

Certainly for the person in crisis for whom such a faith and its celebration has had some meaning, even though this meaning may not in the past have been one of high emotional impact or constant conscious awareness, there is a way in which these symbols may reach deep into the person's life and stimulate hidden resources, reminding him of the larger context of meaning within which he as a human being exists, bringing a strengthening, stabilizing power.

A Lay Crisis Ministry

In addition to the possibilities for the person in crisis growing out of the nature of religious faith itself and participation in the community of faith as it exists in its usual forms of life together, including that of simple personal friendship and support, there is a generally untapped source of power in specifically selected and trained lay persons who have much to give by way of help to other members of the congregation and to the larger community which the congregation also serves.

Lay persons have always exercised a number of functions in the church, ranging from the trivial and dispensable to those of great significance and without which congregational life would disintegrate. However, other than their own spontaneous responses as individuals and families to other individuals and families as they have themselves deemed appropriate, and some of the

[7] *Ibid.*

routine (routine does *not* mean unimportant) pastoral care functions by assignment, such as visiting shut-ins or occasionally the hospital, their potential helpfulness in many of the areas of severe human need has not ordinarily been utilized. One occasionally hears of a congregation that has developed a program of lay pastoral care, but these are exceptional. Why should this be? While only a small percentage of lay persons would have the training necessary to enter into long-term counseling with a person with chronic problems, congregations are full of persons who are relatively mature, have good judgment, can relate well to others, who themselves have experienced a variety of life's stresses and have come through these successfully, and who genuinely care for others. An increasing accumulation of experience and a growing body of some precise data based on this experience have demonstrated that such persons, with only a small amount of training, can be extremely helpful in assisting persons in crisis, from mild to severe, and in other situations of need. Lay volunteers are being effectively used all over this country and in many other countries of the world at the present time in a number of different types of settings in ways that are useful to persons in distress: crisis intervention and suicide prevention centers, mental health clinics, psychiatric hospitals, day care centers, and others. The overall positive results are without question.

It should be made very clear that this is not the attempt to make low level psychiatrists and psychologists. It does mean, however, that it is possible to capitalize on a person's natural humanity, his own particular personality strengths, to help other persons in a number of forms of crisis accomplish significant changes in their

271

lives.[8] It is high time that the religious community drew on its own personnel to meet the vast needs of a hurting humanity.

We ministers, if we have not already done so, will need to shift our understanding of some of the ways in which we approach our tasks in the church and our relationships to the people of our congregations. The day when we viewed ourselves as the only persons rendering pastoral care or engaging in important crisis counseling is past. If we find ourselves at all reluctant to share significant tasks in the congregation with lay persons, we should examine our motivation very carefully. It has been all too common that we have assayed our own value by the amount of work that we have done, and in order to do so have needed to guard some functions as belonging exclusively to ourselves. While this may have given us certain satisfactions, it has often exhausted us, and besides, is heretical. If we have competence in the pastoral care area (or any other, for that matter) our time and energies will be better spent in the selection, training, and supervision of lay persons to share this ministry.

While this procedure will probably neither save time nor decrease the minister's load, the benefits both to him and the congregation will be many. His own work will be multiplied and the congregation will receive a greater amount of supportive care from a greater number of persons. The pastor will also receive the satisfactions from teaching others to function in important areas of the life of the congregation as his own knowledge and skills are sharpened by the training and supervision process. Finally, as a continual by-product, there is the opportunity to educate an entire congregation as

[8] Carkhuff, *Helping and Human Relations*, Vol. I, p. 6.

to the nature of the community of faith, the true nature of the laity, and the mutual ministry that persons committed to God owe one another by virtue of this commitment.

The necessary steps for the effective functioning of a lay counseling program involve the developing of clear-cut plans as to the functions which lay persons will be carrying out, and then their selection, training, and supervision.

Functions. The way in which the minister may use the lay men and women may differ considerably from one setting to another. Most congregations, even relatively small ones, could probably use hospital visitors and visitors for the sick in their homes. Other possibilities are the assignment of an individual or a couple to a person or family in grief or to work with the pastor in a grief work group. Some might be on call for individual emergency crisis counseling sessions either by phone or by visit to the suffering person. Someone might specialize in supporting and guiding the person undergoing divorce or during the period immediately following the divorce. Since the move of a household from one community to another often initiates a crisis reaction, particularly in the wife, especially if she is not working, and also in the children of a family, a group of women might be developed to visit regularly newcomers in the area. These plans, of course, will depend on the needs of the congregation and community, the availability of the persons to do the work, and the ability of the minister either himself or assisted by other professionals, to do the selection, training, and supervision.

Selection. Careful and enlightened selection procedures are absolutely crucial. The public asking for volunteers could be disastrous, unless the pastor has the procedures and is willing to suffer the consequences of a rigorous evaluation and screening process with the result that some number of people will have to be told that they are not acceptable for this program. Certainly everyone who might volunteer would not be the sort of person who could do this work effectively. It is much more efficient and causes less stir for the minister to acquaint himself thoroughly with the personal characteristics necessary for a good helping person and then through his intimate knowledge of the congregation specifically ask certain individuals and couples to assume this responsibility as their major gift of time to the church. While this method is not foolproof, it is probably better than any other, if the minister is at all perceptive and knows his people well. In addition, the training itself should be of such a nature that it will serve as a further screening process, with some people discovering for themselves that they should withdraw from the program.

Several studies give important guidelines as to the necessary characteristics that a person should possess in order to utilize the training most completely and work with persons in crisis in the most helpful way. (As these characteristics are reviewed briefly, it might even be well for the minister to be evaluating himself by them, and if he feels that there are barriers to his own most competent functioning, he may want to seek the assistance of another professional in facilitating his own growth as a person and a professional.)

Carkhuff reports a study which refers to "sincere regard for others, tolerance and ability to accept people with values different from one's own, a healthy regard for the self, a warmth and sensitivity in dealing with

others, and a capacity for empathy." [9] The "healthy
regard for the self" as a factor has been substantiated
in a study in which forty-five crisis center directors responded to an adjective checklist as a means of evaluating their most and least effective volunteers, defined in
terms of their actual performance in handling crisis
calls on the telephone. The checklist did discriminate
between the two groups, with the most significant factors statistically being the higher scoring of the effective
volunteers on self-confidence and dominance and their
low scoring on abasement. They have, apparently, a
more positive view of themselves and what they have to
give in a relationship and feel that they have more control over what happens in their relationships with others
than do the least effective workers. [10] The study of volunteer workers at the Los Angeles Suicide Prevention
Center identified the following as the important criteria
for helping persons: maturity, responsibility, the willingness to accept training and supervision, the ability to
get along well in a group, motivation in terms of wanting
to work directly with people and to learn and develop
personally, and a willingness to give time and effort
consistently over a long period.

Persons who are clearly unsuited for this work were
identified as those who were looking for a way to gratify
their own needs (as distinguished from a legitimate desire to *grow* as a person) and to push their own particular interpretations of human problems and specific
solutions to them. Naturally, rigid persons who cannot
adjust to new situations, who are hypercritical and defensive are unacceptable. [11]

[9] *Ibid.*, p. 8.
[10] Steve Gerard, "Personality Associated with 'Good Volunteers,'"
Crisis Intervention, IV (1972), 90-92.
[11] Sam M. Heilig, Norman L. Farberow, Robert E. Litman, Edwin

The minister must be very aware of these criteria for selection and apply them rigorously as he makes his decisions about whom to invite. He must not allow other personal feelings to influence his evaluations. This program is not a place simply to have one's friends, regardless of their personal characteristics, or to include individuals in a helping project as a means of trying to help them. They must be persons whose impact on others is consistently therapeutic.

Training. The training should best take place in a small group setting. An appropriate beginning point would be to explore in the group the individuals' motivations for responding to the minister's invitation, what they believe they have to offer, their fears and misgivings, how they feel about physical illness and hospitals, death and dying, how they have reacted at funerals, their feelings about suicide, how they typically react in the presence of strong emotion. This exploration, while important, must not consume an excessive amount of time, since the training program is much more than an encounter group. At this point, a very useful procedure should be followed if at all possible. It is the one presented in detail by Carkhuff, based upon highly sophisticated and well-developed exercises designed to improve one's empathetic sensitivities and communications.[12] These exercises are not effective, however, in the hands of a person who is not himself empathetic and who has not undergone this type of training. The minister will need to find someone to lead this section,

S. Shneidman, "The Role of Non-Professional Volunteers in a Suicide Prevention Center," *Community Mental Health Journal*, IV (February, 1968), 289.

[12] *Helping and Human Relations*, Vol. I. pp. 93-133. See also pp. 149-213.

or find a place where he may go through these exercises under expert guidance and then lead the group himself, or simply omit the exercises. He may always, of course, read the relevant materials and discuss with the groups the necessary ingredients of all helping relationships with some benefit to the participants if they have been well selected initially.[13]

Additional input would self-evidently include crisis theory, crisis counseling procedures, and techniques of intervention. The methodology would be some combination of reading, lecture, listening to tapes of crisis counseling sessions, case study, and discussion. Specific problem areas such as physical and mental illness (the latter including an emphasis on depression), grief, family and divorce crises, suicide, and others that may be pertinent for the particular tasks of the lay group of this particular congregation. Obviously, the matter of confidentiality, its meaning and its necessity, will be discussed.

At this time the analysis of crisis counseling tapes, if such are available, and role play become extremely important. Persons must begin to experience what it feels like to be in the helping situation and forced to make specific verbal responses and develop a therapeutic plan for an individual in crisis. The situations should vary according to the specific assignments the lay counselors may later take and also should prepare them to respond flexibly to new situations they might encounter. The anxiety level of participants tends to rise during these sessions and some may decide to withdraw. Great sensitivity on the part of the pastor is needed here as he talks with each of these persons individually, walking the fine line between assisting them

[13] *Ibid.*, Vol. I, pp. 35-39, 173-95; Vol. II, 82-95.

first, to understand that the rise in anxiety is normal and that this alone is not sufficient cause to withdraw, and second, that if their feelings are intense enough and continue to get in the way of their helpful responses, he must be able to expedite their resigning from the program in such a way that they will not feel as if they are failures to themselves or to the church. It is clear that not every person can do this sort of work. For those who withdraw, it might be quite helpful to have a few less threatening pastoral care functions than those of crisis for them to move into, helping them to realize that these other areas of helpfulness are also necessary and important and that their training for the most part will be quite relevant.

Finally whenever possible, the lay trainees should be able to observe real situations similar to those they will be called upon to perform. Some of these may be easily provided, such as a lay person accompanying the minister on several hospital or grief calls. In some cities it might be possible to work out an arrangement with a telephone crisis service for the church trainees to observe for a shift or two. The minister will need to use his ingenuity at this point.

It should be noted that this type of training program includes aspects of self-exploration and growth in self-understanding, exercises that lead to greater empathy and empathic communication and some sense of familiarity with a feeling of doing the work itself, as well as instructional sessions of a more traditional didactic method. Summarized in this way, it becomes obvious that this could describe a year or more of full-time training. However, for the *pre-work* lay crisis pastoral care program in a church, it may be anywhere from twenty to forty hours, depending upon the specific assignments to be assumed. If it is hospital visitation alone, it may be on the lower end of the number of hours, if some face-to-face emergency work, the upper end.

It is important to emphasize that this is the pre-work training. There will be supervision of the work as it is actually done later which forms the foundation of continuing training. Naturally, too little preparation would be unthinkable, but if the training period is too long, especially in *extent* of time more than total hours, people usually begin to lose interest and motivation. An hour a week for forty weeks would probably kill the program, whereas two or three hours a week for twelve to fifteen weeks has been demonstrated to be quite workable. Some experimentation with occasional larger blocks of time has also been attempted with some success, such as two or three Sunday afternoons and evenings of five or six hours each (the experiential beginnings) a few weekly sessions of didactic material, and a couple of several-hour sessions of tape analysis and role play to conclude.

Supervision—continuing training. It is an absolute necessity for the minister, and some other professional if one may be found to volunteer his or her services, to be available on call to the lay persons after they have begun to work. From time to time their own anxieties and feelings of inadequacy, frustration, and even sense of failure will arise, and they will need the opportunity to talk these out as soon as they are being experienced. It will also be important for them to discuss with the pastor or another professional details of a particular person's life or an interpersonal situation and their own functioning in that context. The minister should be able to understand the significance of this type of availability to his workers as being a most efficient use of his own time, since the crisis ministry to persons is being greatly expanded. He will also begin to experience some of the satisfactions and benefits of the supervisory role himself.

In addition to supervision on a personal basis, there may also be occasional group meetings of the lay persons for didactic input, for discussion and fellowship among themselves, and for case presentation and study.

Conclusion. Such a lay crisis care and counseling program will expand and upgrade the pastoral ministry of the congregation to itself and the larger community. The minister will be using his time more efficiently, and while serving as a leader will discover that he himself is learning more and obtaining new satisfactions from his job. The total congregational life will be lifted by the constant example of a high level lay ministry and by the presence in its whole life together of a cadre of people who are increasingly sensitive to other human beings in both the formal and informal meetings of the congregation. The lay crisis helpers will experience great satisfaction for themselves as they become aware of developing sensitivities to others and insight into themselves and as they experience their own significant role in the lives of individuals, families, and the congregation as their expression of ministry to their Lord.

CONCLUSION

This book has sought specifically to focus on the dynamics of individual and family crisis, with its purpose being to upgrade the level of effectiveness of the minister in this important aspect of his pastoral work. The bulk of the material has also been relevant to the role of the minister as the leader in the selection, training, assignment, and supervision of lay persons to do some of this work as their faith commitment, thereby increasing the breadth of his own ministry and competence in his own skills and deepening his satisfaction in his own calling.

The intent of the book has not been to diminish the importance of any other function of the ministry or of any other phase of congregational life. Indeed, the whole center of the life of the community of faith is the context for, stimulus to, and support of crisis ministry: congregational worship, with Word and sacrament; the education of children, youth, and adults; the prophetic Word to the larger community, including direct involvement in social change which involves the creation of a climate in which the well-being of persons is maximized.

Not only crisis ministry itself should be broader than the emergency services such as this book has dealt with, as Jernigan has so well pointed out,[1] but the total pur-

[1] "Pastoral Care and the Crises of Life," pp. 57-64.

pose for the existence of the community of faith is broader than that of present human crisis, although the relationship of major developmental and situational crises to the experience of personal faith and the forms of the community of faith is obvious: birth-creation-baptism; personal and social growth-education in the faith; puberty-personal faith decision-confirmation; love-marriage-celebration; death-grief-resurrection-funeral.

The congregation participates in the life of its Lord when we, ordained clergy and laity alike, commit ourselves to a "being for others" which we understand to be the characteristic attitude of God in relation to us. This means that human distress and suffering and agony cause agony to us, as we have been shown in faith that they do to God himself, and our only effective response is to be moved to action on their behalf. This means that in some way the love of God is literally expressed to persons through those meaningful relationships and communications and activities that are called pastoral care, of which the crisis ministry is one important aspect. This book is a response to the call to the community of faith to be more self-consciously aware of certain forms of intense human need, of the inherent link between who we are called to be as God's people and our ministry to those in crisis, and to commit ourselves to the highest level of helping possible, realizing that this is one form of our seeking to express the love of God.

INDEX OF NAMES

INDEX OF SUBJECTS